BASIC KOREAN:
A GRAMMAR AND WORKBOOK

Basic Korean: A Grammar and Workbook comprises an accessible reference grammar and related exercises in a single volume.

This workbook presents twenty-five individual grammar points in lively and realistic contexts, covering the core material which students would expect to encounter in their first year of learning Korean. Grammar points are followed by examples and exercises which allow students to reinforce and consolidate their learning.

Basic Korean is suitable for both class use as well as independent study.

Key features include:

- abundant exercises with full answer key
- all Korean entries presented in Hangul with English translations
- subject index.

Clearly presented and user-friendly, *Basic Korean* provides readers with the essential tools to express themselves in a wide variety of situations, making it an ideal grammar reference and practice resource for both beginners and students with some knowledge of the language.

Andrew Sangpil Byon is Associate Professor at the State University of New York at Albany, where he teaches courses in Korean language and civilization.

Other titles available in the Grammar Workbooks series are:

Basic Cantonese
Intermediate Cantonese

Basic Chinese
Intermediate Chinese

Basic German
Intermediate German

Basic Italian

Basic Irish
Intermediate Irish

Basic Polish
Intermediate Polish

Basic Russian
Intermediate Russian

Basic Spanish
Intermediate Spanish

Basic Welsh
Intermediate Welsh

BASIC KOREAN:
A GRAMMAR AND
WORKBOOK

Andrew Sangpil Byon

Routledge
Taylor & Francis Group

LONDON AND NEW YORK

First published 2009
by Routledge
2 Park Square, Milton Park, Abingdon, Oxon OX14 4RN

Simultaneously published in the USA and Canada
by Routledge
270 Madison Ave, New York, NY10016

Routledge is an imprint of the Taylor & Francis Group, an informa business

© 2009 Andrew Sangpil Byon

Typeset in Times Ten by Graphicraft Limited, Hong Kong

Printed and bound in Great Britain by
CPI Antony Rowe, Chippenham, Wiltshire

British Library Cataloguing in Publication Data
A catalogue record for this book is available from the British Library

Library of Congress Cataloging-in-Publication Data
Byon, Andrew Sangpil.
  Basic Korean : a grammar & workbook / Andrew Sangpil Byon. – 1st ed.
      p. cm. – (Grammar workbook series)
    1. Korean language – Grammar – Problems, exercises, etc.
    2. Korean language – Textbooks for foreign speakers – English.   I. Title.
  PL913.B96 2008
  495.7′82421–dc22
  2008006927

ISBN10 0-415-77487-X (pbk)
ISBN10 0-203-89227-5 (ebk)

ISBN13 978-0-415-77487-1 (pbk)
ISBN13 978-0-203-89227-5 (ebk)

CONTENTS

PREFACE

Korean-as-a-foreign-language (KFL) teaching and learning in the English-speaking world has hardly been popular among non-Koreans until quite recently. However, the number of KFL learners has started to grow rapidly since the latter half of the 1970s for various reasons, such as the increasing visibility of South Korea on the international stage because of its fast economic development and its democratization over the last four decades, the continuing support from the Korean government regarding the expansion of the Korean Studies program abroad, the growing importance of the North Korean issues in contemporary global-political affairs, and the recent growth of the Korean-American population in the USA.

In the USA alone, the number of colleges that offer KFL courses was merely ten in 1975. However, that number has grown to over 130 in the early 2000s. A few universities, including the University of Hawaii at Manoa and the University of California at Los Angeles, have offered Korean language BA, MA, and PhD programs. The number of Korean community schools (for K-12 Korean and culture education) grew from seven in 1975 to 832 in 1996, and to over 900 in the early 2000s. In addition, over 20 public high schools have recently started to teach Korean. The Korean language boom is not confined within the US private sector or university settings but is found in the government sector as well. For example, US government institutes such as the Defense Language Institute, the Foreign Service Institute, and the Central Intelligence Agency provide intensive Korean language training.

In recent decades the number of KFL textbooks for English-speaking KFL classroom use has steadily increased. However, the number of KFL study materials intended for a self-study purpose is still relatively scarce. Furthermore, to date there has been no published KFL grammar workbook that specifically aims at providing supplemental grammar explanations and exercises in a single volume.

Basic Korean: A Grammar and Workbook and its sister volume, *Intermediate Korean*, are intended to meet that need. The book focuses on providing an accessible reference grammar explanation and related exercises in a single volume. It is designed for independent English-speaking adult KFL learners who intend to maintain and strengthen their knowledge of essential Korean grammar and for classroom-based learners who are looking for supplemental grammar explanations and practices. Consequently, this book differs from existing KFL materials whose primary purpose is to help KFL learners acquire four language skills, such as listening, speaking, reading, and writing, as well as cultural knowledge.

The layout of this book also differs from those of existing KFL materials. For instance, a typical KFL textbook chapter may include model dialogues, followed by vocabulary lists, grammar explanations, cultural notes, and exercises. In contrast, following the pattern of other Grammar Workbooks of the Routledge series, every unit of *Basic Korean* focuses on presenting jargon-free and concise grammar explanations, followed by relevant grammar exercises.

This book has 25 units, and it does not take a functional-situational approach in grouping and/or sequencing target grammatical points. Rather it sequences and covers grammatical points according to their grammatical categories (e.g., nouns, pronouns, particles, numbers, verbs, adjectives, and so on), so that learners can use the book for reference material as well as for practice material. The exercises at the end of each unit are designed primarily to reinforce the target grammatical points.

All Korean entries are presented in Hangul (the Korean alphabet) with English translations to facilitate understanding. Accordingly, it requires that learners familiarize themselves with Hangul in Unit 1, before going on to the rest of the book. In addition, when translating Korean entries into English, efforts were made to reflect the Korean meaning as closely as possible. Consequently, some learners may feel certain English translations do not reflect typical English usages. However, the direct translation approach was employed for pedagogical purposes.

In writing this book, I have been fortunate to have the assistance and support of many people. I would like to thank my colleagues in the Department of East Asian Studies at the University at Albany, State University of New York, who were supportive of this project. I am grateful to anonymous reviewers for their constructive and valuable comments. I would like to express sincere gratitude to Sophie Oliver for initially encouraging this project and to the editorial and production teams at Routledge, Andrea Hartill, Ursula Mallows, Samantha Vale Noya, and Andrew Watts for their advice and support throughout the process. My thanks also go to Lisa Blackwell for her careful and thoughtful copy-editing. Finally, as always, my special thanks go to my wife, Isabel, who, with her optimism and encouragement, makes it possible for me to do what I really love to do. Of course, I bear all responsibility for any shortcomings and errors remaining.

UNIT 1
Reading Hangul (the Korean alphabet)

The Korean writing system "Hangul" is one of the most scientific and systematic writing systems in the world. Hangul is made of an alphabet of 21 vowel and 19 consonant symbols. The system was invented in 1443 by the King Sejong the Great and his group of royal scholars during the Chosun dynasty of Korea (1392–1910). This unit introduces how to read Hangul. The unit introduces individual vowel and consonant symbols and discusses how each symbol is assembled into syllables to spell Korean words.

Vowels

Hangul has a total of 21 vowel symbols. Among them are 11 basic vowel and ten double-vowel symbols. The basic vowel symbols include:

ㅏ	a (as in f<u>a</u>ther)
ㅓ	uh (as in <u>uh</u>-oh)
ㅗ	o (as in h<u>o</u>me)
ㅜ	oo (as in b<u>oo</u>)
ㅡ	u (as in p<u>u</u>ll)
ㅣ	ee (as in f<u>ee</u>t)
ㅐ	a (as in c<u>a</u>re)
ㅔ	e (as in m<u>e</u>t)
ㅚ	we (as in w<u>e</u>t)
ㅟ	wi (as in <u>we</u> are the world)
ㅢ	ui (u as in p<u>u</u>ll, followed by ee as in f<u>ee</u>t, but said quickly as one sound).

Ten double-vowel symbols are made of either adding one more stroke to some of the above basic vowel symbols or combining some basic vowel symbols together. For instance, the following six double-vowel symbols are results of adding one more stroke (adding the y sound) to the first six vowel symbols above (e.g., adding a stroke to ㅏ "a," you get ㅑ "ya").

ㅑ   ya (as in y<u>a</u>rd)
ㅕ   yo (as in y<u>o</u>nder)
ㅛ   yo (as in y<u>o</u>ga)
ㅠ   yu (as in y<u>ou</u>)
ㅒ   ya (as in y<u>a</u>nkie)
ㅖ   ye (as in y<u>e</u>s)

Another four double-vowel symbols are made up of combining some of the basic vowel symbols together (e.g., combining ㅗ "o" and ㅏ "a" produces ㅘ "wa"):

ㅘ   wa (as in w<u>i</u>ne)
ㅝ   wo (as in w<u>o</u>nder)
ㅙ   wae (as in w<u>ai</u>t)
ㅞ   whe (as in w<u>he</u>n)

Notice that the above four double-vowel symbols have the *w* sound.

You may wonder whether other vowel symbols can be combined. However, there are vowel symbols that cannot be combined together. For instance, ㅗ does not combine with ㅓ or ㅔ, whereas ㅜ does not combine with ㅏ or ㅐ. The reason is attributed to the Korean vowel harmony principle.

In Korean, two vowel symbols ㅏ and ㅗ are called "bright vowels" since they sound sonorous to Korean native speakers. Since the vowel symbols such as ㅙ, ㅘ, ㅐ, and ㅒ were derived from ㅏ and ㅗ (e.g., either adding a stroke or combining them together), these vowel symbols are also considered "bright vowels." On the other hand, ㅓ and ㅜ are considered "dark vowels" along with ㅝ, ㅞ, and ㅖ. Meanwhile ㅣ and ㅡ are called "neutral vowels." The vowel harmony principle prohibits the combination of bright and dark vowel symbols.

Consonants

Hangul has 19 consonant symbols, as shown below:

ㅂ   p (as in <u>p</u>ark, but relaxed)
ㅍ   p (as in <u>p</u>ill, aspirated; or with puffs of air)
ㅃ   p (as in s<u>p</u>eak, tense)

ㄷ   t (as in <u>t</u>all, but relaxed)
ㅌ   t (as in <u>t</u>alk, aspirated)
ㄸ   t (as in s<u>t</u>eam, tense)

ㄱ   k (as in <u>k</u>iss, but relaxed)
ㅋ   k (as in <u>k</u>ing, aspirated)
ㄲ   k (as in s<u>k</u>ill, tense)

ㅈ   ch (as in <u>ch</u>ill, but relaxed)
ㅊ   ch (as in <u>ch</u>ange, aspirated)
ㅉ   tch (as in mi<u>dg</u>et, tense)

ㅁ   m (as in <u>m</u>other)
ㅇ   ng (as in ki<u>ng</u>)

ㄴ   n (as in <u>n</u>ose)
ㄹ   l (l as in <u>l</u>ung or r as in Spanish r)
ㅎ   h (as in <u>h</u>ope)

ㅅ   s (as in <u>s</u>oul)
ㅆ   s (as in <u>s</u>ea)

How to combine consonant with vowel symbols

The basic unit of a Korean letter is a syllable. In other words, a complete Korean written letter must have at least one consonant and a vowel symbol. The combinations of the vowel and consonant symbols are fivefold.

First, a syllable consists of only one vowel sound (e.g., like English "a"). Although the letter pronunciation is consisted of only vowel pronunciation like "a" (without any spoken consonant), you still need to start the syllable with a consonant symbol to make the letter complete. For this purpose, you use a Korean consonant ㅇ. The use of the ㅇ symbol is special in that it is used as zero-value consonant when it appears before a vowel. It functions as a place holder in a word-initial position, so that the letter "a" should be written in Korean as 아 (not ㅏ). Let us take another example. Writing a letter for the sound "yo" should look like 요 not ㅛ. Again, although the letter begins with the vowel pronunciation "yo" (without any spoken consonant), you still have to start with a zero-value consonant ㅇ to make it a complete letter, as in 요.

Second, it can have a vowel but followed by a consonant (e.g., like English "on" or 온 in Korean). Third it can have a consonant, followed by a vowel (e.g., like English "go" or 고 in Korean). Fourth, a syllable letter can have a consonant, followed by a vowel, and then a consonant (e.g., like English "dam" or 담 in Korean) or two consonants (e.g., like English "host" or 홓 in Korean).

The position of the vowel symbols is either to the right of or below the initial consonant symbol, as in 미 and 노. If the syllable has a consonant after a vowel symbol, it is always below the vowel, as in 민 and 녹.

There are a few things to remember. First, a Korean syllable does not start with two consonants (e.g., unlike the English word "clip"). In addition, the syllable with three symbols (consonant-vowel-consonant(s)) seems to be more crowded and compacted than the one of two symbols (consonant-vowel) formation. However, each syllable should look about the same size, no matter how many symbols it may contains. For instance, notice that the sizes of the following two letters are about the same: 나 and 흙. Another thing to remember is that Hangul follows the spelling convention, and consequently, Korean spellings do not change just because it reads a little differently from its symbol combinations. In other words, one should not write just as each word sounds (this is the same for English, where you cannot write just as you hear or speak).

Exercises

Exercise 1.1

Among the following vowel symbols, circle the one that is pronounced differently from the others.

데, 다, 대

Exercise 1.2

Among the following vowel symbols, circle the one that is pronounced differently from the others.

괘, 괴, 귀

Exercise 1.3

Among the following vowel symbols, circle the one that is not one of the "bright vowels."

ㅏ, ㅐ, ㅕ, ㅗ, ㅐ, ㅒ

Exercise 1.4

Among the following vowel symbols, circle the one that is not one of the "dark vowels."

ㅜ, ㅕ, ㅖ, ㅘ, ㅓ, ㅖ

Exercise 1.5

The following Korean words are the English borrowed words used in Korean. Match each Korean word with one of the following English words (camera, jazz, taxi, romance, hot dog, Starbucks, quiz, coat, bus, sandwich, hamburger, and coffee):

1 버스
2 커피
3 코트
4 재즈
5 퀴즈
6 로맨스
7 택시
8 스타벅스
9 핫도그
10 샌드위치
11 햄버거
12 카메라

Exercise 1.6

The following are names of countries in Hangul. Make a guess and write the English name for each country.

1 브라질
2 스페인
3 노르웨이
4 핀란드
5 필리핀
6 이탈리아
7 프랑스
8 잉글랜드
9 캐나다
10 멕시코

Exercise 1.7

The following are names of cities in Hangul. Make a guess and write the English name for each city.

 1 뉴욕
 2 시드니
 3 샌프란시스코
 4 런던
 5 파리
 6 서울
 7 마드리드
 8 라스베가스
 9 뉴델리
10 리스본

Exercise 1.8

Match each English name of the country with the corresponding Korean name from the following list:

포르투갈, 사우디 아라비아, 뉴질랜드, 아르헨티나, 이집트, 인디아, 러시아, 오스트레일리아, 이스라엘, 헝가리.

 1 Russia
 2 Egypt
 3 Portugal
 4 Hungary
 5 Saudi Arabia
 6 New Zealand
 7 Argentina
 8 India
 9 Australia
10 Israel

Exercise 1.9

Match each English name of the city with the corresponding Korean name from the following list:

오슬로, 헬싱키, 모스크바, 로마, 토쿄, 상하이, 방콕, 카이로, 멕시코시티, 리오데 자네이로.

 1 Shanghai
 2 Cairo
 3 Rio de Janeiro
 4 Tokyo

5 Moscow
6 Helsinki
7 Rome
8 Oslo
9 Bangkok
10 Mexico City

Exercise 1.10

The following are the names of some world famous people. Make a guess
and write their names in English.

1 지미 카터
2 조지 부쉬
3 애브래햄 링컨
4 조지 와싱턴
5 윈스턴 처칠
6 토마스 애디슨
7 빌 클린턴
8 리오나르도 다빈치
9 엘비스 프레슬리
10 존 레논

Exercise 1.11

The following English words are used as loanwords in Korean. Match the
corresponding Korean words from the following list:

스키, 쿠키, 나이프, 펜, 모니터, 텔레비젼, 카드, 팝송, 바나나, 피자,
오렌지, 샴푸.

1 monitor
2 shampoo
3 pizza
4 ski
5 television
6 pen
7 card
8 cookie
9 pop song
10 knife
11 banana
12 orange

UNIT 2
Characteristics of the Korean language

Word order

English is a subject-verb-object (SVO) language (e.g., Andrew-studies-Korean). However, Korean is a subject-object-verb (SOV) language (e.g., 앤드류가 한국어를 공부해요 "Andrew-Korean-studies"). In Korean, verbs and adjectives appear at the end of the sentence. All other elements such as nouns (e.g., subject and/or object), adverbs, and numbers, appear before verbs and/or adjectives. In addition, modifiers (e.g., adverbs, demonstratives, and relative clauses) appear before the modified words.

For instance, let us consider the following English sentence: "Peter studies history at the library in the afternoon." We know that "Peter" is the subject since it comes before the verb "studies," and "history" is the object as it appears after the verb. Notice that extra elements such as "at the library" and "in the afternoon" are placed after the object. In addition, English prepositions always appear before nouns, as in "at the library."

However, the word order of Korean would be 피터가 도서관에서 역사를 공부해요 "Peter library-at history studies." Instead of English prepositions, Korean has particles that always come after the noun. For instance, we know 피터 is the subject, since it is marked by the subject particle 가. 도서관 is the location since it is marked by the locative particle 에서. In addition, 역사 is the object, since it is marked by the object particle 를.

Consider another example:

앤드류가 집에서 점심을 먹어요 "Andrew eats lunch at home"

The subject particle 가 marks 앤드류 as the subject of the sentence. The location particle 에서 marks 집 as the location. In addition, the object particle 을 marks 점심 as the object of the sentence.

Because of particles, Korean sentences do not always follow the SOV pattern. Korean nouns (as subjects or objects) can be freely arranged in a sentence. For instance, the following six sentences mean "Andrew eats lunch at home."

앤드류가 집에서 점심을 먹어요 "Andrew home-at lunch eats"
앤드류가 점심을 집에서 먹어요 "Andrew lunch home-at eats"
집에서 앤드류가 점심을 먹어요 "Home-at Andrew lunch eats"
집에서 점심을 앤드류가 먹어요 "Home-at lunch Andrew eats"
점심을 앤드류가 집에서 먹어요 "Lunch Andrew home-at eats"
점심을 집에서 앤드류가 먹어요 "Lunch home-at Andrew eats"

The fact that Korean nouns can be freely arranged differs from English, since the English word order typically determines grammatical relationships. The word order affects the Korean language only when certain particles are missing in given sentences (often during the colloquial usages).

Meanwhile, for delimiting the meaning of the nouns, the tone is often used in English. In Korean, however, the changing word orders (e.g., moving the important elements near the verb and less essential elements to the front of the sentence) or using the special particles (e.g., topic particle 은/는) delimit the meanings of nouns.

Context-oriented language

In Korean the most important elements tend to cluster to the end of the sentence. The further the word is from the end of the sentence, the less important the element is and more likely it is to be dropped. In other words, what appears at the very end of the sentence (e.g., verbs) is most important. Consequently, Korean sentences that have no subject or object but just a verb or an adjective, such as in 먹어요 "eat," are grammatically correct and natural in conversation. Here are more examples.

안녕하십니까? "How are you?"
are peaceful

뭐 공부하세요? "What do you study?"
what study

감사합니다 "Thank you"
thanks do

Notice that none of the above expressions contains the first or second person pronoun. What determines the omission is the context. The Korean language is a context-oriented language in that any contextually understood elements may be omitted unless they are indispensable.

General-to-specific language

Korean is a "general-to-specific" or "big-to-small" language. In other words, Koreans write or say general, or bigger, units before the specific, or smaller, units. For instance, Koreans say or write the last name before the given name (e.g., 김정민 "Kim Jungmin").

When writing an address, they write the name of the country, followed by the province, city, street, house number, and the name of the receiver.

대한민국, 경기도, 서울시, 금천구, 독산동 113, 김정민
(Republic of Korea, Kyonggi Province, Seoul, Kumchon-District, Toksan 113, Kim Jungmin)

When writing a date, the year comes first, followed by month and the day.

2007 년 8 월 5 일   (2007-year 8-month 5-day)

Honorific language

Korean is an honorific language in that it has grammatical elements that are used to indicate social meanings involved in contexts such as speakers' attitudes (e.g., respect, humility, formality) toward who they are talking to or talking about.

For instance, Koreans use hierarchical address-reference terms of titles as well as various speech levels to indicate politeness, intimacy, and the formality level of discourse during interaction. In addition, they use humble person pronoun forms such as 저 "first person singular" and 저희 "first person plural" to indicate humility. Moreover, Koreans use honorific suffix -(으)시 and euphemistic words to indicate respect toward a subject of higher social status. The following examples illustrate how Korean honorifics work:

(a) 어제 우리 모임에 와 주어서 고마워
     "(I) appreciated that you came to our meeting yesterday."
(b) 어제 저희 모임에 와 주시어서 고맙습니다.
     "(I) appreciated that you came to our meeting yesterday."

As seen above, the referential meanings of the two sentences are the same. However, their social meanings are different. For example, in (a), the use of the plain first person pronoun, 우리, the absence of the honorific suffix -시, and the use of an intimate speech level -어 indicate that the speaker is likely addressing a person either of equal (=power) or lower status (-power), and whom he/she knows well (-distance). Because it lacks proper honorific elements, the example in (a) would be rude in a formal situation if it was used by a lower-status person (e.g., a college student) addressing a higher-status person (e.g., a professor).

To make (a) socially appropriate in a +power situation (e.g., talking to someone of higher status), one should change 우리, first person plural genitive pronoun, to 저희, humble first person plural genitive pronoun, as shown in (b). In addition, one should add the honorific suffix -시 to the gerundive verb 주어서 "giving (me)" making 주셔서 thereby transforming it into an honorific verb, and use the deferential speech level sentence-ending 습니다 to change 고마워 "thanked (you)" to 고맙습니다, in the deferential speech level. The above examples illustrate how the use of honorifics in Korean functions as a social indicator. In addition, they demonstrate that how an utterance is said is more important than what is said.

Exercises

Exercise 2.1

Circle whether the following statements are True or False.

> Example: in English, prepositions always appear before nouns, as in *at home.* (**T** / F)

1 In Korean, verbs and adjectives appear at the end of the sentence. (T / F)
2 In Korean, nouns, adverbs, and numbers, appear after verbs and/or adjectives. (T / F)
3 In Korean, what appears at the very beginning of the sentence is most important. (T / F)
4 In Korean, word order typically determines grammatical relationships. (T / F)
5 Instead of English prepositions, Korean has particles that always come before nouns. (T / F)
6 Korean sentences do not always follow the SOV pattern. (T / F)
7 Word order affects the Korean language only when certain particles are missing in sentences. (T / F)
8 Korean sentences that have no subject or object but just a verb are grammatically correct and natural in conversation. (T / F)
9 In Korean, different forms of expressions are used depending on who you are talking to or talking about. (T / F)

Exercise 2.2

Write each component of the sentence in the SOV word order.

    Example: 한국어를 (the Korean language) 공부해요 (studies)
                    수잔이 (Susan)
                    = 수잔이 한국어를 공부해요

 1 조깅 해요 (jogs), 마이클이 (Michael), 운동장에서 (at track).
 2 조앤이 (Joan), 먹어요 (eats), 점심을 (the lunch).
 3 농구를 (basketball), 티모티가 (Timothy), 해요 (plays).
 4 텔레비전을 (television), 봐요 (watches), 브루스가 (Bruce).
 5 마크가 (Mark), 만들어요 (makes), 스파게티를 (spaghetti).
 6 자요 (sleeps), 집에서 (at home), 다이앤이 (Diane).
 7 이야기해요 (talks), 필립한테 (to Philip), 캐롤이 (Carol).
 8 커피를 (coffee), 테디가 (Teddy), 마셔요 (drinks).
 9 학교에 (to school), 가요 (goes), 찰스가 (Charles).
10 토니가 (Tony), 쳐요 (plays), 피아노를 (piano).

Exercise 2.3

Arrange the following elements according to the Korean convention.

    Example: July 18, 2007
                = 2007, July 18.

1 December 24, 2005
2 Sumi Kim
3 712-19 Hankuk Street, Jung District, Seoul, Kyonggi Province, Republic of Korea.
4 Daesung Lee
5 18 May, 1977
6 Kyonggi Province, Republic of Korea, Kangnam District, 81-3 Taehan Street, Seoul

UNIT 3
Nouns

Words and word classes

Words are basic units that constitute a sentence. Each word in a sentence has different functions. Based on its grammatical function, each word is categorized into different classes, such as nouns, verbs, adjectives and so on. Korean has the following word classes.

1 Nouns
2 Pronouns
3 Particles (that attach to a noun and indicate grammatical relationships or add special meanings)
4 Numbers and counters
5 Verbs (that indicate action or progress)
6 Adjectives (that indicate state or quality)
7 Copula (that indicate an equational expression: 이다 "be" and 아니다 "be not")
8 Adverbs
9 Prenouns (that appear before a noun, like English demonstratives such as this, that, these, and those)

These Korean words in general fall into two categories: inflected words and uninflected words. Inflection refers to the process of adding some kinds of affixes to the original word in order to indicate grammatical features such as tense, number, aspect, and person. The addition of the affixes changes the shape of the original word in the process; however, it does not change its form class.

For instance, in English, the word "go" becomes "goes" with the affix "-es" when it is used for a third person singular. Another example is when the verb "study" changes its form to "studied" with the affix "-ed." The process of adding such affixes refers to inflection. Notice that these inflected verbs end up having additional grammatical features (e.g., the third person verb usage and past tense) but their class does not change (e.g., they are still verbs).

In Korean, the category of words that undergoes inflection includes verbs and adjectives. On the other hand, the category of words that does not undergo inflection includes nouns, pronouns, numbers, adverbs, and prenouns. All of these different classes of words will be discussed in detail throughout this book. However, this unit focuses on nouns. Nouns in general refer to the part of speech that indicates a name of thing, quality, place, person, or action. Nouns often serve as the subject and/or object of verbs and/or adjectives.

Formation of nouns

There are three components that constitute Korean nouns: native Korean words (about 35 percent); Sino-Korean words (about 60 percent), and loan words (about 5 percent). Generally speaking, Korean nouns can be comprised of either a single morpheme (or a meaningful unit), such as 나무 "tree," 산 "mountain," 새 "bird," 물 "water," or multiple morphemes (e.g., a combination of several single morphemes) such as 화산 "volcano" (화 "fire" + 산 "mountain") and 소고기 "beef" (소 "cow" + 고기 "meat").

Nouns consisting of more than two morphemes are normally formed through either a derivational or a compounding process. The derivational formation takes an affix (e.g., either a prefix or a suffix), which normally appears in a noun and/or a predicate (e.g., a verb and/or an adjective). Prefixes refer to the affixes that appear before the word, whereas suffixes refer to the affixes that appear after the word.

Derivational prefixes:
- Native Korean prefix (e.g., 맏 "first")
  - 맏아들 "the first son" = 맏 "first" + 아들 "son"
  - 맏딸 "the first daughter" = 맏 "first" + 딸 "daughter"
- Sino-Korean prefix (e.g., 신 "new")
  - 신학기 "a new semester" = 신 "new" + 학기 "semester"
  - 신인 "a new comer" = 신 "new" + 인 "person"

Derivational suffixes:
- Native Korean suffix (e.g., 꾼 "doer")
  - 장사꾼 "business man" = 장사 "business" + 꾼 "doer"
  - 일꾼 "worker" = 일 "work" + 꾼 "doer"
- Sino-Korean suffix (e.g., 학 "study")
  - 한국학 "Korean studies" = 한국 "Korea" + 학 "study"
  - 수학 "mathematics" = 수 "number" + 학 "study"
- Nouns, derived from verbs (e.g., 이/기 "act")
  - 벌이 "income" = 벌 "earn" + 이 "act"
  - 먹기 "eating" = 먹 "eat" + 기 "act"

- Nouns, derived from adjectives (e.g., 이/기 "quality")
  - 크기 "size" = 크 "big" + 기 "quality"
  - 길이 "length" = 길 "long" + 이 "quality"

As seen above, derivation is a useful way to understand how a word can be developed into another word with an affix, which carries an additional meaning.

On the other hand, compound nouns consist of two or more independent morphemes. They are divided into native and Sino-Korean compound nouns:

Native compound words:
- noun + noun
  - 눈물 "tears" = 눈 "eye" + 물 "water"
  - 물개 "seal" = 물 "water" + 개 "dog"
- adverb + noun
  - 곱슬머리 "curly hairs" = 곱슬 "curved" + 머리 "hair"
  - 산들바람 "gentle breeze" = 산들 "gentle" + 바람 wind"
- noun + predicate + nominalizer
  - 목걸이 "necklace" = 목 "neck" + 걸 "hang" + 이 "act"
  - 본보기 "model" = 본 "example" + 보 "look" + 기 "act"
- predicate + noun
  - 늦잠 " oversleeping" = 늦 "late" + 잠 "sleeping"
  - 고드름 "icicle" = 곧 "straight" + 얼음 "ice"
- clause + noun
  - 찬물 "cold water" = 찬 "cold" + 물 "water"
  - 못난이 "stupid person" = 못난 "ugly" + 이 "person"

Sino-Korean compound words
- Sino-Korean word + Sino-Korean word
  - 부모 "parents" = 부 "father" + 모 "mother"
  - 천지 "universe" = 천 "heaven" + 지 "earth"

Meanwhile, Korean has a group of special nouns that always appear before other nouns to modify or describe the following nouns, such as 무슨 음식 "<u>what kind of</u> food," 이 책 "<u>this</u> book," 그 사람 "<u>that</u> man," and 어느 식당 "<u>which</u> restaurant." These nouns are called "prenouns" (like English words, such as "that," "this," and "which").

Some nouns are used only after the aforementioned prenouns. These special nouns (also sometimes called "bound nouns") cannot be used by themselves but used always with the prenouns. Examples of these nouns are 이 곳 "this <u>place</u>," 그 분 "that <u>person</u>," 저 것 "that <u>thing</u>," and so on. Prenouns as well as bound nouns are discussed in detail in Unit 22.

Some characteristics of Korean nouns

Marking plurality

English is very specific with respect to number in that when there is more than one item, the item must be marked by the plural "s." However, Korean nouns are not specific about the number in that it does not have the grammatical category of number. For instance, a Korean noun 연필 "pencil" can be translated into at least the following: pencil, a pencil, the pencil, some pencils, the pencils, and pencils. Korean has the suffix 들 (that can be attached after a countable noun) for indicating the plurality of the noun. However, its usage is not mandatory for marking plurality, thus its purpose is rather for highlighting the plurality of the noun.

Position of nouns

Korean nouns appear in a sentence in one of the following ways: (1) by itself, (2) before particles, (3) before another noun, and (4) before copula. For instance, consider the following sentence:

선생님, 수잔이 미국 대학생이에요 "Teacher, Susan is an American college student"

Notice that 선생님 "teacher" appears by itself; 수잔 "Susan" appears with the subjective particle 이; 미국 "America" appears before another noun 대학생 "college student"; 대학생 appears before 이에요 "copula."
   The Korean copula (or be-verbs such as "am," "is," and "are") is 이다 (or 이에요 with the polite speech level). Korean nouns can serve as the sentence predicate with the copula. For instance, consider the following sentence: 톰이 학생이에요 "Tom is a student." What is noteworthy is that the copula attaches to the noun so tightly as if it were a particle. For example, notice that there is no space between 학생 and 이에요, as in 학생이에요.

Noun usage with verbs

People tend to use nouns with certain verbs. For instance, in English, the word "crime" is collocated with the verb "commit," and "operation" is collocated with the verb "perform." The use of a noun with a verb that is not conventionally collocated (although the use of the verb may be grammatically correct) results in an awkward expression (e.g., "Hitler committed a crime" vs. "Hitler performed a crime"). In the same principle, Korean nouns tend to collocate with certain verbs.

Consider the following examples:

레베카가 농구를 놀아요 "Rebecca plays basketball" (X)
레베카가 농구를 해요 "Rebecca plays (lit. does) basketball" (O)

The verb 놀아요 literally means "play," and 해요 means "do." However, in Korean, the noun 농구 "basketball" does not collocate with 놀아요, but with 해요. For playing musical instruments such as piano and guitar, a different verb 쳐요 "play" or "hit" is used instead of 해요 or 놀아요.

레베카가 피아노를 놀아요 "Rebecca plays piano" (X)
레베카가 피아노를 해요 "Rebecca plays (lit. does) piano" (X)
레베카가 피아노를 쳐요 "Rebecca plays (lit. hits/plays) piano" (O)

Exercises

Key vocabulary for Unit 3 exercises

가 the edge
개 dog
계란 egg
고기 meats
고무 rubber
고무신 rubber shoes
나물 greens
돌 stone/pebble
문 door
물 water
물개 seal

바늘 needle
바다 sea
바닷가 the seaside
방 room
빵 bread
빵집 bakery
벽 wall
벽돌 brick
부채 fan

사업 business
산나물 wild edible greens
새 bird

신 shoes
앞 front
앞문 font door
음악 music
철 season
철새 migratory bird
책 book
책방 book store
코 nose
코피 blood from the nose
피 blood

Exercise 3.1

Translate the following Korean words into English:

Example: 사람   <u>people</u>

1 새   _____
2 사업   _____
3 부채   _____
4 벽   _____
5 고기   _____
6 계란   _____
7 바늘   _____
8 고무   _____
9 나물   _____
10 음악   _____

Exercise 3.2

The following are compound words. Write their English meanings.

Example: 닭고기
          <u>Chicken (meat)</u> = <u>닭 Chicken</u>   + <u>고기 meat</u>

1 고무신   _____ = _____ + _____
2 산나물   _____ = _____ + _____
3 벽돌   _____ = _____ + _____
4 앞문   _____ = _____ + _____
5 코피   _____ = _____ + _____
6 바닷가   _____ = _____ + _____

7	빵집	_____	=	_____	+	_____
8	책방	_____	=	_____	+	_____
9	물개	_____	=	_____	+	_____
10	철새	_____	=	_____	+	_____

Exercise 3.3

The Korean nouns in each set have the same prefix. Identify the prefix
and give its meaning.

Example: 날고기 (raw meat), 날생선 (raw fish), 날계란 (uncooked egg)
= Prefix: 날   Meaning: <u>raw</u>

1 신학기 (new semester), 신세대 (new generation), 신형 (new model)
Prefix:_____ Meaning: _____
2 고급 (high class), 고가 (high price), 고도 (high degree), 고산 (high
mountain)
Prefix:_____ Meaning: _____
3 불가능 (impossible), 불가피 (unavoidability), 불감증 (insensibility),
불공평 (unfairness), 불규칙 (unsteadiness)
Prefix:_____ Meaning: _____

Exercise 3.4

The Korean nouns in each set have the same suffix. Identify the suffix
and give its meaning.

Example: 소설가 (novelist), 음악가 (musician),
사업가 (businessman)
Suffix: <u>가</u>   Meaning: <u>person</u>

1 한국식 (Korean style), 미국식 (American style), 중국식 (Chinese
style)
Suffix:_____ Meaning: _____
2 바느질 (sewing), 가위질 (scissoring), 부채질 (fanning)
Suffix:_____ Meaning: _____
3 교직 (teaching profession), 기술직 (skill-related profession), 성직 (the
ministry)
Suffix:_____ Meaning: _____

UNIT 4
Predicates and endings

Predicates

Predicate, one of the main components of a sentence, normally refers to the part that explains or says something about the subject. Often it refers to a verb or an adjective phrase that modifies the subject. For example, "closed the door" is the predicate of a sentence "Peter closed the door." In a similar manner, those which constitute predicate expressions in Korean are verbs and adjectives.

Stems

Korean verbs and adjectives are made of stems and endings. The stems of verbs and adjectives do not stand alone, and they are always conjugated by various or inflectional endings. These endings carry various grammatical information and roles (e.g., tense, aspect, speech levels, and so forth).

When you look for the meaning of certain verbs and/or adjectives in your dictionary or textbook word lists, you are most likely to encounter verbs and adjectives with 다 as their endings (e.g., 자다 "sleep," 놀다 "play," and 어렵다 "difficult"). Remember that stems do not stand by themselves. For a dictionary-entry purpose, Korean verbs and adjectives take a special dictionary form ending -다. Consequently, finding the stem of a verb and/or an adjective is simple in that anything being left out after you take 다 out from the verbs and adjectives is the stem. Here are some examples:

Dictionary form	Meaning	Stem
가다	go	가
먹다	eat	먹
배우다	learn	배우
요리하다	cook	요리하
나쁘다	bad	나쁘
작다	small	작
좋다	good	좋
아름답다	beautiful	아름답

Verbs and adjectives

In English, one can distinguish a verb from an adjective by looking at their structure. For example, when using an adjective as a predicate, one has to use one of "am," "is," and "are" (e.g., "the book is cheap"). In Korean, however verbs and adjectives resemble one another in how they inflect and how they function in the sentence. In addition, there is no obvious structural difference between verbs and adjectives. In fact adjectives behave like verbs so much that Korean grammarians categorize adjectives as "descriptive verbs."

For example, in a dictionary, you may find the following Korean verb and adjective: 가다 "go" and 작다 "small." They have different stems (가 and 작) but the same ending (다 the dictionary form ending). Their meanings distinguish a verb from an adjective. Verbs normally signify actions and processes. On the other hand, adjectives typically indicate states or qualities (e.g., size, weight, quality, quantity, shape, appearance, perception, and emotion).

Vowel- and consonant-based stems

Stems of Korean verbs and adjectives are grouped into two types: consonant based and vowel based. An example of the vowel-based stem is 가 of 가다, whereas that of the consonant-based stem is 먹 of 먹다.

Vowel-based verbs
가르다	"divide"
가지다	"have"
가르치다	"teach"
만지다	"touch"
보다	"see"
배우다	"learn"
타다	"ride"

Consonant-based verbs
닫다	"close"
신다	"wear (shoes)"
받다	"receive"
살다	"live"
앉다	"sit"
읽다	"read"
팔다	"sell"

Vowel-based adjectives

시다	"sour"
싸다	"cheap"
쓰다	"bitter"
짜다	"salty"
크다	"big"
흐리다	"cloudy"
희다	"white"

Consonant-based adjectives

가볍다	"light (weight)"
가깝다	"near"
괜찮다	"fine"
넓다	"wide"
많다	"many"
작다	"small"
좋다	"good"

Endings

Since the stems of verbs and adjectives cannot be used alone, they are always used with endings. Korean has many different endings that convey much of the grammatical functions such as tense, aspects, sentence types, conjunctions, speech levels, and so on.

The endings can be categorized into two types: pre-final endings and final endings, depending on where they are placed in the verb or adjective.

Pre-final endings

Pre-final endings are inflectional elements that come between the stem and the final ending. They include the honorific suffix -(으)시, past tense marker 었/았, and so on.

Consider the following example:

어제 영화 보<u>시었</u>어요? "Did (you) see the movie yesterday?"

Notice that the pre-final endings (e.g., 시 and 었) appear between 보, the stem "see," and 어요, "a sentence final ending."

Non-sentence-final endings

There are two types of final endings: one that ends a verb or an adjective but not the sentence (non-sentence-final endings), and one that ends both the verb and the sentence (sentence-final endings). Non-sentence-final endings include various clausal conjunctives such as -고 "and then," -어/아서 "because," -으면서 "while," -지만 "although," -도록 "in order to," and so on.

Consider the following sentence.

커피를 마시고 아이스크림을 먹어요 "(I) drink coffee, and then eat ice cream"

Notice that the conjunctive -고 "and then" does not end the sentence but does end the verb stem 마시 "drink." On the other hand, the ending 어요 ends the verb "eat" as well as the sentence.

Sentence-final endings

The typical examples of sentence-final endings are various speech-level endings. Korean has six speech levels as shown below. These speech-level endings indicate the speaker's interpersonal relationship with the address-ees or attitude toward them (e.g., social meanings such as intimacy and formality of the situation).

The deferential speech level is the highest among the six, followed by the polite speech level and so on. In addition, each speech level has four endings that indicate the type of sentence: declarative (statement), interrogative (question), imperative (command/request), and propositive (suggestion):

Speech level	Declarative	Interrogative	Imperative	Propositive
1 Deferential	-습니다/ ㅂ니다	-습니까/ ㅂ니까	-(으)십시오	-(으)십시다
2 Polite	-어요/-아요	-어요/-아요	-어요/-아요	-어요/-아요
3 Blunt	-(으)오	-(으)오		
4 Familiar	-네	-나/-는가	-게	-세
5 Intimate	-어/-아	-어/-아	-어/-아	-어/-아
6 Plain	-(느)ㄴ다	-(으)니/-냐	-어라/-아라	-자

Among the six speech levels, the use of (3) blunt and (4) familiar speech levels have been declining especially among young generations. KFL learners however must be familiar with the deferential, polite, intimate, and plain levels, which are still widely used for all Koreans regardless of age differences. Consequently, the debate around blunt and familiar speech levels will not be discussed in this book.

Let us apply four of the endings above to the verb stem 먹 "eat." When saying "(someone) eats," one needs to use one of the four interrogative endings (-습니까, -어요, -어, and -냐).

Level	Conjugation	Possible social settings
Deferential	먹습니까? "(Someone) eats?"	(e.g., in a formal situation)
Polite	먹어요? –	(e.g., to an adult colleague)
Intimate	먹어? –	(e.g., to an adolescent friend)
Plain	먹냐? –	(e.g., to a child)

Notice that the verb stem in each speech level as well as the referential meaning are the same. In addition, different endings render different social meanings, such as speaker's attitude toward the hearer and the formality of the situation. Consequently, choosing the right speech level is critical, and it all depends on who you talk to.

Exercises

Exercise 4.1

The following is a list of some Korean verbs and adjectives. Underline whether it is a verb or an adjective and then write the stem of each verb and adjective.

   Example: 읽다 <u>Verb</u>/Adjective   Stem: 읽

1	가볍다	Verb/Adjective	Stem:_____
2	가지다	Verb/Adjective	Stem:_____
3	팔다	Verb/Adjective	Stem:_____
4	닫다	Verb/Adjective	Stem:_____
5	많다	Verb/Adjective	Stem:_____
6	만지다	Verb/Adjective	Stem:_____
7	타다	Verb/Adjective	Stem:_____
8	앉다	Verb/Adjective	Stem:_____
9	시다	Verb/Adjective	Stem:_____
10	넓다	Verb/Adjective	Stem:_____

Exercise 4.2

Among six speech levels, what are two speech levels whose uses are declining among young generations?

Exercise 4.3

Among six speech levels, what is the level used for formal and public speech?

Exercise 4.4

Apply one of the four declarative endings (-습니다, -어요, -어, and -는다) to the stem of 묶다 "tie."

1 Deferential _____
2 Polite _____
3 Intimate _____
4 Plain _____

Exercise 4.5

Apply one of the four interrogative endings (-습니까, -어요, -어, and -니) to the stem of 넣다 "place (something) in."

1 Deferential _____
2 Polite _____
3 Intimate _____
4 Plain _____

Exercise 4.6

Apply one of the four propositive endings (-ㅂ시다, -어요, -어, and -자) to the stem of 배우다 "learn."

1 Deferential _____
2 Polite _____
3 Intimate _____
4 Plain _____

Exercise 4.7

Apply one of the four imperative endings (-으십시오, -어요, -어, and -어라) to the stem of 읽다 "read."

1 Deferential _____
2 Polite _____
3 Intimate _____
4 Plain _____

UNIT 5

The deferential speech level and the polite speech level

In English, there are times when you have to take alternative words or phrases, depending on various social factors involved in conversation, such as the formality of the situation, politeness, and familiarity with the addressee. For instance, in a certain situation, you can greet someone by saying "Hey, what's up!" but in another situation by saying "Good morning, Sir!"

Korean has different speech level endings for serving these purposes. As already emphasized in the previous unit, the use of speech level endings is mandatory all the time, since verb or adjective stems cannot stand alone. However, for Korean language learners, choosing an appropriate speech level ending for every verb and/or adjective is challenging because its selection is determined by various contextual factors involved in interaction, such as who you are talking to, whether you know the addressee or not, how formal the situation is, and so on. The focus of this unit is on two speech levels: "the deferential speech level" and "the polite speech level."

The deferential speech level

The deferential speech level is used for public and/or formal communication settings, such as broadcasting, public speech, business-related meetings, conference presentations, and so forth. The deferential speech level has four different endings for each sentence type: -습니다/-ㅂ니다 (declarative), -습니까/-ㅂ니까 (interrogative), -(으)십시오 (imperative), and -(으)십시다 (propositive).

Declarative

For the declarative (statement), -습니다 is used when the stem ends in a consonant, as in 먹 + 습니다 = 먹습니다 "(someone) eats." However, when the stem ends in a vowel, -ㅂ니다 is used, as in 가 + ㅂ니다 = 갑니다 "(someone) goes."

Because the deferential speech level indicates a sense of formality, many formulaic/fixed expressions are made of this speech level ending:

처음 뵙겠습니다	"Nice to meet you" (literally, "(I) meet you for the first time")
만나서 반갑습니다	"Nice to meet you" (literally, "(I) am glad because I meet you")
잘 먹겠습니다	"Thanks for the meal" (literally, "(I) will eat well")
감사합니다	"Thank you" (literally, "(I) do gratitude")
실례합니다	"Excuse me" (literally, "(I) do discourtesy")
축하합니다	"Congratulations" (literally, "(I) congratulate")

Interrogative

For the interrogative (question), the ending is -습니까 for the stem ending in a consonant, as in 먹습니까? "(do you) eat?" However, it is -ㅂ니까 for the stem ending in a vowel, as in 갑니까? "(do you) go?" Here are more examples.

굽다 "roast"	언제 고기를 굽습니까? "When (do you) roast the meat?"
믿다 "believe"	그 친구를 믿습니까? "(Do you) believe that friend?"
가르치다 "teach"	어디서 한국어를 가르칩니까? "Where (do you) teach Korean?"
배우다 "learn"	언제 태권도를 배웁니까? "When (do you) learn Taekwondo?"

Imperative

For the imperative (command), the ending is -으십시오 for the stem ending in a consonant, as in 먹으십시오 "eat." However, the ending is -십시오 for the stem ending in a vowel, as in 가십시오 "go." Here are more examples.

닫다 "close"	창문을 닫으십시오 "Close the window"
읽다 "read"	한국어 책을 읽으십시오 "Read the Korean book"
만나다 "meet"	선생님을 만나십시오! "Meet the teacher!"
보다 "see"	코미디 영화를 보십시오! "See the comedy movie!"

Propositive

For the propositive (suggestion), the ending is -으십시다 for the stem ending in a consonant, as in 먹으십시다 "(let us) eat." However, it is

-십시다 for the stem ending in a vowel, as in 갑시다 "(let us) go." Here are more examples.

끊다 "quit"	담배를 끊읍시다 "(Let us) quit smoking"
앉다 "sit"	앞줄에 앉읍시다 "(Let us) sit in the front row"
보내다 "send out"	편지를 보냅시다 "(Let us) send out the letter"
버리다 "throw away"	쓰레기를 버립시다 "(Let us) throw away the garbage"

The polite speech level

The polite speech level is the informal counterpart of the deferential speech level. As the most commonly used speech level regardless of age or gender, the polite speech level is broadly used in any situation where polite language is called for. It is used when addressing someone of senior status in a casual, non-formal, and everyday types of conversations; it is used with friends if their friendship began in adulthood; it is the most common speech level used toward strangers.

The polite speech level endings have two forms: -어요 and -아요. When the verb and/or adjective stem ends in either 아 or 오, -아요 is used. On the other hand, -어요 is used with the stem that ends in any other vowels. For example, the following is a list of some verbs and adjectives (with dictionary endings) in the left column with the polite speech level ending -어/아요 in the right column:

Dictionary form	The polite speech level endings
가다 "go"	가요 (가 + 아요 but contracted to 가요)
보다 "see"	봐요 (보 + 아요 but contracted)
오다 "come"	와요 (오 + 아요 but contracted)
받다 "receive"	받아요 (받 + 아요)
살다 "live"	살아요 (살 + 아요)
기다리다 "wait"	기다려요 (기다리 + 어요 but contracted to 기다려요)
배우다 "learn"	배워요 (배우 + 어요 but contracted)
넣다 "put (something) in"	넣어요 (넣 + 어요)
묶다 "tie"	묶어요 (묶 + 어요)
먹다 "eat"	먹어요 (먹 + 어요)

You probably wonder why some verbs or adjectives such as 가다 is not 가아요, but 가요. This is attributed to the vowel contraction in Korean: when similar or the same two vowels appear together (e.g., 가아 = 가), the vowels tend to be contracted.

The copula 이다 "be" and 아니다 "be not" as well as the verb 하다 "do" do not follow the above rules. The conjugation of 이다, 아니다, and 하다 is irregular in that the polite speech level of 이다 is 이에요, 아니다 is 아니에요, and 하다 is 해요.

이다	이어요 (X)	이에요 (O)
아니다	아니어요 (X)	아니에요 (O)
하다	하아요 (X)	해요 (O)

The endings -어/아요 are used for all sentence types: declarative, imperative, interrogative, and propositive. For instance, consider the following:

점심을 먹어요 "(I) eat lunch"
점심을 먹어요? "(Do you) eat lunch?"
점심을 먹어요! "Eat lunch!"
점심을 먹어요. "(Let us) eat lunch"

Koreans use contextual elements as well as intonation (e.g., rising intonation for a question) to figure out what sentence type the ending is used for.

Mixed use of the deferential and polite speech levels

Koreans frequently use the deferential speech level as well as the polite speech level together even in formal conversational settings. One possible scenario is when you meet a person for the first time. The speakers may introduce themselves using the deferential speech level (using the aforementioned fixed expressions). However, once identified, they may switch to the polite speech level. The use of the polite speech level ending generates an effect of making a dialogue sound less formal, even in formal conversational contexts.

Exercises

Key vocabulary for Unit 5 exercises

가게 store
가르치다 to teach
건너다 to cross over
공 ball
구두 shoes

그리다 to draw
그림 painting
기다리다 to wait
기분 feeling
기차 train
기회 chance
길 road
깨끗하다 to be clean

날씨 weather
내려가다 to go down
느리다 to be slow
닫다 to close
달다 to be sweet
담배 cigarette
대학생 college student
던지다 to throw
두드리다 to knock
따르다 to follow
뜨겁다 to be hot (water)

마시다 to drink
마치다 to finish
매일 everyday
먹다 to eat
멀다 to be far
문 door
물 water
물고기 fish
믿다 to believe
밑 bottom

바쁘다 to be busy
받다 to receive
방 room
배 stomach
배우다 to learn
버리다 to throw away
버스 bus
보내다 to send
보다 to see; to watch
빌리다 to borrow

선생님 teacher
손 hand
숙제 homework

쉽다 to be easy
쓰레기 garbage
시험 test
시끄럽다 to be noisy
신다 to wear (shoes)
싱싱하다 to be fresh
씻다 to wash

아니다 not be
아침 morning
아프다 to be hurt
앉다 to sit
야채 vegetable
어디 where
언제 when
여기 here
열다 to open
영어 English
영화 movie
일 work
일어나다 to get up
일찍 early
읽다 to read
입다 to wear (clothes)

자다 to sleep
잡다 to catch
재미있다 to be interesting
점심 lunch
좋다 to be good
주다 to give
지갑 wallet
집 house
찾다 to find
책 book
춥다 to be cold
친구 friend
커피 coffee
코메디 comedy
코트 coat
크게 aloud
타다 to ride
택시 taxi

팔다 to sell
편지 a letter

피우다 to smoke
하늘 sky
하다 to do
학교 school
한국 사람 Koreans
한국어 the Korean language
헤어지다 to be separated/break up
흐리다 to be cloudy

Exercise 5.1

Conjugate each verb or adjective with the deferential speech level ending (declarative) and translate each sentence.

Example: 학교에 (가다)
= 학교에 갑니다 "(I) go to school"

1 점심을 (먹다)
2 한국어를 (가르치다)
3 친구를 (기다리다)
4 커피를 (마시다)
5 편지를 (받다)
6 영어를 (배우다)
7 방이 (깨끗하다)
8 기차가 (느리다)
9 물이 (뜨겁다)
10 매일 (바쁘다)

Exercise 5.2

Conjugate each verb or adjective with the deferential speech level ending (interrogative) and translate each sentence.

Example: 학교에 (가다)
= 학교에 갑니까? "Do (you) go to school?"

1 언제 가게 문을 (닫다)
2 어디서 손을 (씻다)
3 언제 (앉다)
4 어디서 (자다)
5 담배를 (피우다)
6 지갑을 (찾다)

   7 날씨가 (춥다)
   8 시험이 (쉽다)
   9 기분이 (좋다)
  10 집이 (시끄럽다)

Exercise 5.3

Conjugate each verb or adjective with the deferential speech level ending
(imperative) and translate each sentence.

> Example: 학교에 (가다)
> = 학교에 가십시오 "Please go to school"

   1 길을 (건너다)
   2 밑으로 (내려가다)
   3 공을 (던지다)
   4 문을 (두드리다)
   5 선생님을 (따르다)
   6 친구를 (믿다)
   7 구두를 (신다)
   8 코트를 (입다)
   9 손을 (잡다)
  10 크게 (외치다)

Exercise 5.4

Conjugate each verb or adjective with the deferential speech level ending
(propositive) and translate each sentence.

> Example: 학교에 (가다)
> = 학교에 갑시다 "(Let us) go to school"

   1 편지를 (보내다)
   2 그림을 (그리다)
   3 물고기를 (잡다)
   4 책을 (읽다)
   5 일을 (마치다)
   6 버스를 (타다)
   7 여기서 (헤어지다)
   8 코미디 영화를 (보다)
   9 기회를 (주다)
  10 쓰레기를 (버리다)

Exercise 5.5

Underline which of the two English translations below is the correct version of the Korean in each case:

Example: 버스를 탑시다
"(Let us) take a bus"/"Take a bus"

1 Page 5 를 읽으십시오.
   "(Let us) read page 5"/"Read page 5."
2 손을 씻읍시다.
   "Wash hands"/"(Let us) wash hands."
3 창문을 닫으십시오.
   "(Let us) close the window"/"Close the window."
4 책을 빌립시다.
   "(Let us) borrow the book"/"Borrow the book."
5 도서관에서 나가십시오.
   "Go out from the library"/"(Let us) go out from the library."
6 물을 마십시오.
   "Drink water"/"(Let us) drink water."
7 음식을 줍시다.
   "(Let us) give (them) food"/"Give (them) food."
8 유니폼을 입으십시다.
   "Wear the uniform"/"(Let us) wear the uniform."
9 한국어를 배우십시오.
   "Learn the Korean language"/"(Let us) learn the Korean language."
10 서울로 떠납시다.
   "(Let us) leave for Seoul"/"Leave for Seoul."

Exercise 5.6

Conjugate each verb or adjective in parenthesis with the polite speech level ending and translate the sentence, as shown in the example:

Example: TV 를 (보다)
          = TV 를 봐요 "(I) watch TV"

1 길을 (건너다)
2 문을 (열다)
3 책을 (팔다)
4 쓰레기를 (버리다)
5 문을 (닫다)
6 일을 (마치다)

 7 책을 (빌리다)
 8 손을 (씻다).
 9 아침에 일찍 (일어나다)
10 택시를 (타다)
11 집이 (좋다)
12 영화가 (재미있다)
13 한국 사람 (이다)
14 숙제를 (하다)
15 대학생이 (아니다)
16 학교가 (멀다)
17 커피가 (달다)
18 배가 (아프다)
19 하늘이 (흐리다)
20 야채가 (싱싱하다)

UNIT 6
The subject case particle 이/가 *i/ka*

Case and special particles

One unique characteristic of Korean is that nouns are typically marked by particles. There is no corresponding equivalent in English. Korean has two types of particles: case particles and special particles. Case particles indicate the syntactic role of the noun to which they are attached (e.g., whether the noun is a subject, an object, an indirect object, and so on). Case particles include 이/가 "subject case particle," 을/를 "object case particle," and so on. Consider the following exemplary sentence:

찰스가 커피를 마셔요 "Charles drinks coffee"

찰스 is the subject, as it is marked by the subject particle 가. In addition, 커피 is the object, as it is marked by the object particle 를.

The other type is "special particles" whose function is not to indicate syntactic roles of the noun but rather to add special meanings, such as indicating the noun as a topic of the sentence, emphasizing the singularity of the noun, and so on. Special particles include 은/는 "topic particle" and delimiters such as 만 "only," 도 "also," and so on. Consider the following example:

차는 현대 소나타가 좋아요 "As for a car, Hyundai Sonata is good"

Notice that 현대 소나타 is the subject of the sentence (since marked by the subject particle 가), while 차 is not the subject but the topic of the sentence (since marked by the topic particle 는).

Characteristics of particles

There are few things to remember when using these particles. First, although particles are tightly bound to and are an integral part of the noun, they can be often omitted in colloquial usages. This omission in colloquial conversation is possible because the contextual understanding of the conversation is often sufficient to indicate the syntactic roles of the nouns being used (e.g., knowing who is a subject or an object and so on). However, the omission of the particles is not allowed in formal written communication.

Second, because of the case particle's role of indicating the syntactic role of the nouns, the word order can be scrambled. For instance, notice that the following two sentences have the same meaning, even if the word order of both sentences (e.g., the subject 찰스 and the object 커피) is different.

찰스가 커피를 마셔요 "Charles drinks coffee"
커피를 찰스가 마셔요 "Charles drinks coffee"

The subject particle 이/가

The subject case particle 이/가 is a two-form particle. 이 is used when the particle comes after a noun that ends in a consonant (e.g., 가방이 "bag-particle"), and 가 is used when the particle comes after a noun that ends in a vowel (e.g., 학교가 "school-particle"). The principle of having two forms resembles the use in English of "a/an." However, the rule is the opposite in that "an" is used before a noun that begins with a vowel (e.g., an umbrella) and "a" is used before a noun that begins with a consonant (e.g., a cup).

The particle 이/가 in negation

Although the primary function of 이/가 is to indicate the subject case, its usage extends beyond case marking. For example, in negation the noun it marks is not the subject of the sentence. Consider the following example:

사라는 한국 사람이 아니에요 "As for Sara, (she) is not a Korean"

사라 is not the subject but the topic of the sentence (as it is marked by the topic particle 는). Notice that the subject of the sentence is omitted, and 한국사람, marked by the particle 이, is not the subject of the sentence.

Double subject constructions

Some Korean sentences may have two nouns marked by the subject particle. Consider the following example:

친구가 세 명이 왔다 "Three friends came"

Notice that there are two subjects in the sentence, 친구 and 세명, as both are marked by the subject particle. Korean grammarians call such a sentence "double-subject construction." Double-subject sentences are very common in Korean. However, its interpretation is not that the sentence has two subjects. In this sentence, the focus is on the number three rather than friends.

Consider another example:

토마스<u>가</u> 손<u>이</u> 크다 "Thomas's hands are big"

In this sentence, the relationship between two nouns, 토마스 and 손, is that of the possessor-possessed.

It is rather confusing which noun marked by the particle should be regarded as the emphasized subject. Koreans use context as well as other linguistic cues (e.g., intonation) to figure out where the emphasis lies. The importance of contextual understanding is also evident in the fact that Korean subjects as well as particles are often omitted in conversation.

Exercises

Key vocabulary for Unit 6 exercises

가깝다 to be near
가격 price
가수 singer
간호사 nurse
강아지 puppy
깨끗하다 to be clean
국 soup
귀엽다 to be cute
기자 journalist
길 road
김치 kimchi
날씨 weather
넓다 to be spacious
달다 to be sweet
더럽다 to be dirty
덥다 to be hot
도서관 library
뜨겁다 to be hot (water)
레몬 lemon

많다 to be many
맛없다 to be tasteless
맛있다 to be delicious
맵다 to be spicy

머리 head
멀다 to be far
목수 carpenter
물 water
미지근하다 to be lukewarm

방 room
비싸다 to be expensive
싸다 to be cheap
설탕 sugar
성격 personality
소금 salt
쉽다 to be easy
스케줄 schedule
쓰다 to be bitter (taste)
시다 to be sour
시험 test
싱겁다 to be bland

아름답다 to be beautiful
앵커우먼 anchorwoman
약 medicine
약사 pharmacist
어렵다 to be difficult
어지럽다 to be dizzy
엔지니어 engineer
영화 movie
영화 배우 movie star
위험하다 to be dangerous
음식 food
의사 medical doctor

자동차 car
짜다 to be salty
짧다 to be short
재미있다 to be interesting
조용하다 to be quiet
좋다 to be good
집 house

차 tea
차갑다 to be cold (water)
초콜릿 chocolate
캠퍼스 campus
커피 coffee
컴퓨터 computer

크다 to be big
펜 pen
학교 school
한국 사람 Koreans
회사원 office worker
흐리다 to be cloudy

Exercise 6.1

The subject particle is a two-form particle: 이 and 가. Fill in the blank with an appropriate subject particle, and translate the sentence.

> Example: 버스 ( ) 있어요
> = 버스(가) 있어요 "There is a bus"

1 토마스 ( ) 있어요.
2 수잔 ( ) 있어요.
3 바바라 ( ) 있어요.
4 앤드류 ( ) 있어요.
5 폴 ( ) 있어요.
6 존 ( ) 있어요.
7 에비 ( ) 있어요.
8 앤서니 ( ) 있어요.
9 캐서린 ( ) 있어요.
10 찰스 ( ) 있어요.

Exercise 6.2

Complete the sentence using the subject particle as shown in the example. Then, translate the sentence.

> Example: 집, 크다
> = 집이 큽니다 "The house is big"

1 영화, 재미있다
2 한국 사람, 많다
3 음식, 맛없다
4 도서관, 조용하다
5 자동차, 비싸다
6 학교, 가깝다
7 성격, 좋다
8 음식, 짜다

Exercise 6.3

Translate the following sentences into English.

> Example: 화장실이 작아요
> = "The toilet is small"

1 학교가 멀어요.
2 방이 깨끗해요.
3 커피가 달아요.
4 한국 음식이 맛있어요.
5 가격이 싸요.

Exercise 6.4

Translate the following sentences into English.

> Example: 날씨가 나쁩니다
> = "The weather is bad"

1 집이 큽니다.
2 강아지가 귀엽습니다.
3 날씨가 덥습니다.
4 시험이 어렵습니다.
5 머리가 어지럽습니다.

Exercise 6.5

Translate the following sentences into Korean using the polite speech level.

> Example: "The size is small"
> = 사이즈가 작아요

1 "The schedule is short."
2 "The pen is expensive."
3 "The house is spacious."
4 "The chocolate is sweet."
5 "The computer is expensive."

Exercise 6.6

Translate the following sentences into Korean using the deferential speech level.

> Example: "The weather is cold"
>   = 날씨가 춥습니다

1 "The weather is cloudy."
2 "The road is dangerous."
3 "The test is easy."
4 "The room is dirty."
5 "The campus is beautiful."

Exercise 6.7

Change each sentence into a negative sentence, as shown in the example.

> Example: 존은 대학생이에요
>   = 존은 대학생이 아니에요

1 일레인은 가수예요.
2 찰스는 엔지니어예요.
3 리디아는 의사예요.
4 제이슨은 기자예요.
5 엔지는 약사예요.
6 브라이언은 회사원이에요.
7 줄리는 간호사예요.
8 사이몬은 목수예요.
9 이사벨은 앵커우먼이에요.
10 톰은 영화 배우예요.

Exercise 6.8

Match one of the following with the appropriate predicates.

스시, 설탕, 소금, 국, 약, 김치, 음식, 커피, 레몬, 물, 차, 초콜릿

   Example: (Sushi) _____이/가 맛있어요
           = 스시가 맛있어요

  1 (chocolate) _____이/가 맛있어요
  2 (sugar)   _____이/가 달아요
  3 (medicine)   _____이/가 써요
  4 (soup)   _____이/가 짜요
  5 (food)   _____이/가 싱거워요
  6 (kimchi)   _____이/가 매워요
  7 (coffee)   _____이/가 뜨거워요
  8 (water)   _____이/가 차가워요
  9 (lemon)   _____이/가 셔요
10 (tea)   _____이/가 미지근해요

UNIT 7
The special particle 은 *ŭn*/는 *nŭn*

The special particle 은/는 is a topic particle since it marks the noun as the sentence topic (e.g., what the sentence is about). The particle 은/는 is not a case particle; hence it does not indicate the grammatical function of the noun it attaches to.

Marking topics

In a similar way that the subject particle has two forms이 and 가, the topic particle also has two forms: 은 (after consonants) and 는 (after vowels). Consider the following two sentences:

> 수잔은 한국 사람이에요 "As for Susan, (she) is a Korean"
> 데니는 미국 사람이에요 "As for Danny, (he) is an American"

Notice that 수잔 is marked by 은 (since it ends in a consonant), whereas 데니 is marked by 는 (since it ends in a vowel). In addition, the above two sentences are "topic-comment" structures: a sentence begins with a topic of the sentence (marked by the topic particle 은/는), followed by the predicate (e.g., an equational expression). In the first sentence above, 수잔 is the topic and 한국 사람이에요 is the comment. In the second sentence, 데니 is the topic, while 미국 사람이에요 is the comment. Such a topic-comment structure is the most basic sentence type in Korean.

To understand its usage in more detail, let us consider the following examples:

> 리아는 미국 사람이에요 "As for Leah, (she) is an American"
> 고등학교 선생님이에요 "(She) is a high-school teacher"
> 28살이에요 "(She) is 28 years old"
> 제임스는 캐나다 사람이에요 "As for James, (he) is a Canadian"

Notice that the first three sentences are about Leah. Because of the fact that Leah was noted as the topic in the first sentence, it would be redundant to raise Leah as the topic again. Consequently, the second and the third sentence omit the topic 리아. However, as the fourth sentence is about a different person 제임스, the sentence begins with the new topic, 제임스.

The noun marked by 은/는 appears to be the subject of the sentence. However, 은/는 is not a subject particle and it does not mark the noun as the subject. For instance, consider the following sentence:

> 햄버거는 스미스 햄버거가 맛있어요 "As for hamburgers, Smith Hamburger is tasty"

Notice that the hamburger is the topic of the sentence (what the sentence is talking about), whereas "Smith Hamburger" is the subject of the predicate "tasty."

Compare and contrast

When two sentences, marked by the topic particles 은/는, are used in parallel, the particle 은/는 serves to compare and contrast the two topics of the sentences. Consider the following two examples:

> 저스틴은 캐나다 사람이에요 "As for Justin, (he) is a Canadian"
> 그렇지만 치에꼬는 일본 사람이에요 "However, as for Chieko, (she) is a Japanese"

Notice that both Justin and Chieko are the topics of each sentence. Since these sentences are used in parallel, these two topics are compared and contrasted (e.g., one is a Canadian while the other person is Japanese).

Switching topics

Koreans use the topic particle 은/는 when they switch the topic from one thing to another. For instance, consider the following conversation.

> A: 실례합니다. 이 바지 얼마예요? "Excuse me, how much is this pair of pants?"
> B: 네. 20,000 원입니다. "Yes, (it) is 20,000 won."
> A: 그럼, 이 치마는 얼마예요? "Then, as for this skirt, how much is (it)?"
> B: 네 32,000 원입니다. "Yes, (it) is 32,000 won."
> A: 이 청바지는요? "How about this pair of jeans?"

Let us assume that speaker A is a customer and speaker B is a saleswoman in the above conversation. Notice that speaker A uses the topic particle 은/는 when she changes the topic from one item to another (e.g., asking for the price of a skirt, and then jeans).

Interplay between the subject and the topic particles

When asking a question in Korean, the question word (e.g., 무엇 "what," 누구 "who") is usually marked by the subject particle 이/가. However, when answering the question, the question word is often marked by the topic particle 은/는. Consider the following examples:

Peter: 전공이 뭐예요? "What is (your) major?"
Susan: 전공은 한국어예요. "As for (my) major, (it) is Korean."

In Peter's question, the particle 이/가 is used since 전공 "major" is the subject of the question. However, when responding to this question, Susan answers 전공은 한국어예요 "As for (my) major, (it) is Korean," instead of 전공이 한국어예요 "The major is Korean." Notice that 전공 is marked by the topic particle 은/는, not the subject particle 이/가.

When Peter asks the question, 전공 is the subject of the sentence and it is not the topic of the conversation yet. In other words, the word 전공 is new information which was just brought up in the conversation. However, after Peter's question, 전공 becomes the topic. As a result, Susan replies with 전공은 rather than 전공이.

This may sound confusing but, it should become clear with more examples. Consider the following examples:

A: 이름이 뭐예요? "What is (your) name?"
B: 제 이름은 앤드류예요. "As for my name, (it) is Andrew."

A: 고향이 어디예요? "Where is (your) hometown?"
B: 제 고향은 서울이에요. "As for my hometown, (it) is Seoul."

Appearing at the beginning of the sentence

You can make any element of the sentence the topic by adding the topic particle to it and placing it at the beginning of the sentence, except the verb/adjective that appears at the end of the sentence. For example, consider the following sentences:

존은 오전 9 시에 메리하고 도서관에서 한국어를 공부해요.
"As for John, (he) studies Korean with Mary at the library at 9:00 a.m."

오전 9 시에는 존이 메리하고 도서관에서 한국어를 공부해요.
"At 9:00 a.m., John studies Korean with Mary at the library."

메리하고는 존이 오전 9 시에 도서관에서 한국어를 공부해요.
"With Mary, John studies Korean at the library at 9:00 a.m."

도서관에서는 존이 오전 9 시에 메리하고 한국어를 공부해요.
"At the library, John studies Korean with Mary at 9:00 a.m."

As a SOV language, in Korean the most important sentential elements (e.g., predicates) tend to appear at the end of the sentence. The less important or least unknown information tend to appear toward the beginning of the sentence. Notice in the above sentences that the 은/는 -marked elements (topics) appear at the beginning of the sentence. The topic of the sentence in Korean tends to be the contextually understood element, and thus it can be often easily omitted during conversation.

This contrasts with the subject marked by the particle 이/가. The subject particle 이/가 is used to mark a subject (which happens to be new information or has not been mentioned previously in the context). For instance, this explains why most interrogative words such as 누구 "who," 무엇 "what," 언제 "when," and 어느 "which," are used with the particle 이/가, as in 누구(가), and 무엇이, but not with the topic particle 은/는:

어느 식당 음식은 맛있어요? "Which restaurant food is delicious?" (X)
어느 식당 음식이 맛있어요? "Which restaurant food is delicious?" (O)

누구는 미국 사람이에요? "Who is an American?" (X)
누가 미국 사람이에요? "Who is an American?" (O)

Exercises

Key vocabulary for Unit 7 exercises

계절 season
꽃 flower
과목 subject/course
날씨 weather
뉴질랜드 New Zealand
러시아 Russia

멕시코 Mexico
봄 Spring
브라질 Brazil
미국 America/USA
색 color
소설 novel

역사 history
영국 England
영화 movie
운동 sport
음식 food
이탈리아 Italy
일본 Japan

자동차 automobile
장미 rose
중국 China
책 book
캐나다 Canada
컴퓨터 computer
코미디 comedy
파랑 blue (color)
프랑스 France
필리핀 Philippines
한국 South Korea
호주 Australia

Exercise 7.1

Complete the sentence using the topic particle and translate the sentence, as shown in the example:

Example: 토마스 / 미국 사람
= 토마스는 미국 사람이에요 "As for Thomas, (he) is an American"

1 유미꼬 / 일본 사람
2 캐서린 / 캐나다 사람
3 왜이 / 중국 사람
4 혜진 / 한국 사람
5 존 / 영국 사람
6 스티브 / 호주 사람
7 루이스 / 프랑스 사람

8 마리오 / 멕시코 사람
9 이반 / 러시아 사람
10 알프레도 / 이탈리아 사람

Exercise 7.2

Complete the sentence using the topic particle and translate the sentence, as shown in the example:

Example: 음식 / 스테이크
= 음식은 스테이크를 좋아해요 "As for food, (I) like steak"

1 음악 / 재즈
2 영화 / 코미디
3 운동 / 야구
4 책 / 한국 소설
5 꽃 / 장미
6 과목 / 역사
7 계절 / 봄
8 색 / 파랑색
9 컴퓨터 / 맥켄토씨
10 자동차 / BMW

Exercise 7.3

Translate the following sentences into Korean.

Example: As for Harry, (he) is in Britain
= 해리는 영국에 있어요

1 "As for Erin, (she) is in Canada."
2 "As for Joshua, (he) is in Mexico."
3 "As for Florence, (she) is in Brazil."
4 "As for Ronald, (he) is in the Philippines."
5 "As for Francis, (she) is in New Zealand."
6 "As for William, (he) is in Russia."
7 "As for Christine, (she) is in France."
8 "As for Charles, (he) is in Italy."
9 "As for Sara, (she) is in China."
10 "As for Michael, (he) is in Japan."

Exercise 7.4

Underline which of the three Korean sentences is the correct translation of the given English sentence:

Example: "As for the book, (it) is at home"
책은 집에 있어요/ 책이 집에 있어요/ 책는 집에 있어요

1 "Who is James?"
누가 제임스예요? / 누구이 제임스예요? / 누구는 제임스예요?
2 "As for color, (I) like white."
색이 흰색을 좋아해요/ 색은 흰색을 좋아해요 / 색는 흰색을 좋아
해요.
3 "As for today's weather, (it) is hot."
오늘 날씨가 더워요 / 오늘 날씨은 더워요 /오늘 날씨는 더워요.
4 "Taxi is expensive."
택시는 비싸요/ 택시가 비싸요 / 택시은 비싸요.
5 "The school is far."
학교는 멀어요/ 학교가 멀어요/ 학교은 멀어요.
6 "As for coffee, hazelnut is delicious."
커피는 해이즐넛이 맛있어요. / 커피가 해이즐넛이 맛있어요 / 커피
은 해이즐넛이 맛있어요.

Exercise 7.5

Choose the right particle for each sentence.

Example: 집(이/가/은/는) 어디예요? "Where is your home?"
= 집이 어디예요?

1 테렌스(이/가/은/는) 3 학년이에요. "Terrence is a junior."
2 스티븐(이/가/은/는) 1학년이에요. "As for Steven, (he) is a freshman."
3 어디(이/가/은/는) 은행이에요? "Where is the bank?"
4 상우(이/가/은/는) 한국 사람이에요. "Sangwoo is a Korean."
5 켄 (이/가/은/는) 일본 사람이에요. "As for Ken, (he) is a Japanese."
6 마리오(이/가/은/는) 멕시코 사람이에요. "As for Mario, (he) is a Mexican."
7 누구(이/가/은/는) 선생님이에요? "Who is the teacher?"
8 자동차(이/가/은/는) 현대(이/가/은/는) 좋아요. "As for cars, Hyundai is good."
9 제 이름 (이/가/은/는) 앤드류예요. "As for my name, (it) is Andrew."
10 제 고향 (이/가/은/는) 서울이에요. "As for my hometown, (it) is Seoul."

UNIT 8
Pronouns

English has an extensive list of pronouns: I (me, my, mine), you (your, yours), he (him, his), she (her, hers), it (its), we (us, our, ours), and they (them, their, theirs). Korean has its own list of pronouns as well, but its usage is much limited with different usage rules. Generally speaking, pronouns are used much less in Korean than in English. In Korean, any contextually understood sentence elements (including the subject and the object) are often omitted. For instance, when two people are talking to each other, personal pronouns often drop out in normal conversations, since both speakers know who is the first person talking and who is listening. This differs from English, where the use of the pronoun (or subject noun) is mandatory in all situations. For instance, it would be grammatically wrong or incomplete to say "ate lunch?"

The first person pronoun

The Korean first person pronouns have the plain and humble forms:

나 (plain singular) 저 (humble singular)
내 (plain singular possessive) 제 (humble singular possessive)
우리 (plain plural/possessive) 저희 (humble plural/possessive)

There are two things to remember when using the first person pronouns. First, the use of either plain or humble pronouns depends on who you are talking to. It is always safe to use the humble form when you talk to adult speakers whom you do not know well. In addition, the use of humble form is normally collocated with honorific elements (e.g., the deferential speech level endings, the honorific suffix -(으)시, the euphemistic words, and so forth).

Second, 저희/우리 "the first person plural pronoun" has a wider usage. Due to the collectivistic value system, deeply embedded in the Korean language and culture, 저희/우리 is also used as the first person possessive pronoun, when referring to communal possessions (e.g., one's family or household, the school he/she attended and so on). Consider the following two sentences:

저희(우리) 형이 뉴욕 올바니에 있습니다 "<u>Our (my)</u> older brother is in Albany, NY"
제 (내) 형이 뉴욕 올바니에 있습니다 "<u>My</u> older brother is in Albany, NY"

Both sentences are grammatically and pragmatically correct. However, the first sentence is preferred over the second.

The second person pronoun

The Korean second person pronouns have the plain and polite forms:

너 (plain singular)	당신 (polite singular)
네 (plain singular possessive)	당신의 (polite singular possessive)
너희 (plain plural)	당신들 (polite plural)

The use of Korean second person pronoun is much more limited than that of English. For example, Koreans use 너 only when addressing a child, a childhood friend, one's younger sibling, one's son/daughter, and so forth. The use of 당신 is mostly used between spouses.

In fact, there is no second person pronoun for addressing an adult equal or senior in Korean. One possible explanation is that addressing someone by the pronoun sounds too direct and confrontational in Korean. As a result, Koreans avoid using the second person pronoun unless the addressee is someone they know well (e.g., friends), and/or is of equal or lower status (e.g., one's subordinates).

One may wonder then how Koreans actually address someone. The safest way is not to use any pronoun at all. However, if unavoidable, the best alternative is to use addressee terms as second person pronouns. As shown below, Korean has many ways to address someone. When using an address term, a speaker has to know the addressee's social status as well as the relationship with the speaker him/herself.

For instance, a businessman 김영수 "Kim, Youngsoo" can be addressed in his work place at least in the following ways:

과장님   "Section chief" (professional title 과장 + honorific title 님, when his junior colleagues address him).
김 과장   "Section chief Kim" (last name 김 + professional title 과장, when his boss addresses him).

김 선배   "Senior Kim" (last name 김 + rank term 선배, when his junior colleague who happens to have graduated from the same high school addresses him).

김영수씨 "Mr. Youngsoo Kim" (full name 김영수 + neutral title 씨, when adult distant friends who are of equal or higher status address him).

Notice that the difference in status (e.g., who has the higher status or power between the speaker and the addressee) and the familiarity (e.g., how close or familiar the speaker is with the addressee/referent) determines the choice of term.

In his personal life, Youngsoo Kim can be addressed by different terms. For instance, his wife may call him 여보 "darling," 당신 "dear," and 오빠 "older brother" (if she is younger than him). If he has a son or a daughter, the wife can even call him 아빠 "dad." His friends can call him by just his first name 영수. His parents can call him by the first name with the vocative -야, as in 영수야.

Then how would you address someone in a store or restaurant settings? Again, the safest way is not to say any pronoun at all. Instead of pronouns, you can get people's attention by saying 여기요 "here" or 실례합니다 "excuse me."

The third person pronoun

Strictly speaking, Korean has no true third person pronoun. Koreans use a demonstrative (e.g., this, these, that, and those) and a noun (e.g., man, woman, thing, people, and so on) to refer to the third person:

He
그 "that," 그 사람 "that person," 그 분 "that esteemed person," 그 남자 "that man" . . .

She
그 "that," 그 사람 "that person," 그 분 "that esteemed person," 그 여자 "that lady" . . .

They
그들 "those," 그 사람들 "those people," 그 분들 "those esteemed people" . . .

Beside these terms, Koreans use various kinship terms in place of the third person pronoun.

Kinship terms

Due to the collectivistic and hierarchical values embedded in the Korean language and culture, Korean has a list of highly stratified and extensive kinship terms. The Korean kinship terms indicate how one is related to others in intricate ways (e.g., whether the relative is a male or female, whether the relative is older or younger, whether the relative is on the mother's or father's side, and so on).

The Korean kinship terms can be divided into two groups. The first group has two kinship term sets depending on the gender of the person related.

	A male's	A female's
father-in-law	장인	시아버지
mother-in-law	장모	시어머니
spouse	아내 (부인)	남편
brothers	형제	오빠들과 남동생들
older brother	형	오빠
older sister	누나	언니

The second group includes the kinship terms, used by both genders.

grandparents	조부모
paternal grandfather	할아버지
maternal grandfather	외할아버지
paternal grandmother	할머니
maternal grandmother	외할머니
parents	부모
father	아버지
mother	어머니
son	아들
daughter	딸
grandchild(ren)	손주
grandson	손자
granddaughter	손녀(딸)
younger brother	남동생
younger sister	여동생
paternal uncle	큰아버지 (an older brother of one's father)
	작은아버지 or 숙부 (a married younger brother of one's father)
	삼촌 (an unmarried younger brother of one's father)
	고모부 (the husband of the sister of one's father)

paternal aunt	고모 (both older or younger sister of one's father)
	큰어머니 (the wife of an older brother of one's father)
	작은어머니 or 숙모 (the wife of a married younger brother of one's father)
maternal uncle	외삼촌 (both older and younger brother of one's mother, regardless of their marital status)
	이모부 (the husband of a sister of one's mother)
maternal aunt	이모 (both older or younger sister of one's mother)
	외숙모 (the wife of both older or younger brother of one's mother)
son-in-law	사위
daughter-in-law	며느리
cousin	사촌

Koreans use kinship terms as both address and/or reference terms for their kin-members. For instance, it is rare for younger brothers or sisters to address their older siblings by their first name.

Due to the collectivistic and hierarchical value orientations of Korean, Koreans use some kinship terms when they address or refer to non-kin members, such as friends, friends' family members, and/or even strangers. For instance, Koreans often use 어머니 when addressing and/or referring to their friends' mother. When addressing a stranger who looks obviously old (say, over 60s), Koreans use 할아버지 or 할머니.

Indefinite pronouns

People use indefinite pronouns when they refer to something that does not have a specific referent. The examples of indefinite pronouns in English include something, someone, sometimes, somewhere, anything, anyone, and so forth. Korean interrogative words such as 어디 "where," 언제 "when," 누구 "who," 무엇 "what," and 어느 "which" function as question words as well as indefinite pronouns. What determines the use of these words as question words or indefinite pronouns is intonation.

When the word is used as a question, the sentence that contains the question word has a rising intonation at the end. However, without a rising intonation, the question word functions as an indefinite pronoun.

As a question word:	누가 와요? (with a rising intonation) "Who is coming?"
As an indefinite pronoun:	누가 와요 (with a falling intonation) "Someone is coming"

Exercises

Key vocabulary for Unit 8 exercises

가방 bag
가족 family
경찰 police
고등학생 high-school student
남편 husband
사무실 office
신발 shoes
전공 major
지갑 wallet
초등학교 elementary school
컴퓨터 computer
회사 company
회사원 office worker

Exercise 8.1

Choose the appropriate first person pronoun for each situation:

Example: A grown up son talking to his old father (나, 저)
= 저

1 A brother talking to his brother (나, 저)
2 A student talking to his/her teacher (나, 저)
3 A boss talking to his/her employees (in public speaking) (나, 저)
4 Employees talking to their boss (우리, 저희)
5 Teenagers talking to their peers (우리, 저희)
6 Businessmen talking to their business partners (우리, 저희)
7 A father talking to a son (나, 저)
8 A husband talking to his wife (나, 저)
9 An adult talking to a child (나, 저)
10 An adult talking to his/her childhood friends (나, 저)

Exercise 8.2

Translate the following into Korean.

Example: My house (an adult talking to his/her friend)
= 우리 집

1 My major (a college student talking to his/her professor)
2 My computer (a college student talking to his/her junior classmate)
3 My family (a college student talking to his/her professor)
4 My older sister (a male adult talking to his friends)
5 My wallet (an adult talking to his friend)
6 My shoes (a teenager talking to her younger brother)
7 My office (a boss talking to his employees, in public speaking)
8 My bag (an adult talking to her senior colleagues)
9 My father (a teenager talking to his/her peers)
10 My company (businessmen talking to their clients)

Exercise 8.3

Choose the most appropriate address term from the choices given in the bracket.

Example: Addressing one's husband (여보/ 너/ 저기요/ name)
= 여보

1 Addressing a server in the restaurant (너/ 자네/ 당신/ 저기요)
2 Addressing a child on the street (너/ 당신/ 자네/ 여보)
3 Addressing one's father (아버지/ 당신/ 너/ 여보)
4 Addressing one's older sister (당신/ 너/ 자네/ 누나)
5 Addressing a stranger who looks in his 70s (당신/ 너/ 자네/ 할아버지)
6 Addressing one's wife (너/ 여보/ 저기요)
7 Addressing one's older brother (형/ 당신/ 여보/ name)
8 Addressing one's childhood friend (너/ 여보/ 당신)

Exercise 8.4

Choose the most appropriate reference term from the choices given in brackets.

> Example: Referring to one's husband (아빠/ 그 분 / 그 남자)
>   = 아빠

1 Referring to his older brother (그 분/ 그 남자/ 그 사람 / 형)
2 Referring to one's grandfather (그 남자 / 그 사람/ 할아버지/ name)
3 Referring to one's best friend's mother (그 남자/ 어머니/ 그 사람 / name)
4 Referring to one's younger sister (그 분/ 그 여자/ 그 사람 / 여동생)
5 Referring to one's father (그 사람/ 그 여자/ 그 분/ 아버지)
6 Referring to his teacher (그 남자/ 그 사람 / 선생님)
7 Referring to a stranger who looks in his 20s (그 사람/ 선생님/ 할아버지)
8 Referring to one's uncle (그 사람/ 그 남자/ 큰아버지)

Exercise 8.5

Underline the gender of each speaker.

> Example: 우리 오빠가 경찰이에요 "My older brother is a policeman"
>   (M / F)
>   = F

1 우리 형이 미국에 있어요 "My older brother is in USA" (M / F)
2 우리 언니가 대학생이에요 "My older sister is a college student" (M / F)
3 우리 오빠가 한국에 있어요 "Our older brother is in Korea" (M / F)
4 우리 누나가 일본에 있어요 "Our older sister is in Japan" (M / F)
5 저희 장모님이 서울에 계세요 "My mother-in-law is in Seoul" (M / F)
6 오늘 저희 시어머니가 오세요 "My mother-in-law comes today" (M / F)
7 저희 시아버지가 미국사람이세요 "My father-in-law is an American" (M / F)
8 우리 남편이 엔지니어예요 "My husband is an engineer" (M / F)

Exercise 8.6

Translate the following into English, as shown in the example.

　　Example:　우리 언니가 고등학생이에요
　　　　　　　 = "My/our older sister is a high-school student"

1　저희 할아버지가 공무원이셨어요.
2　저희 아버지가 회사원이세요.
3　저희 어머니가 초등학교 선생님이세요.
4　저희 작은아버지가 엔지니어이세요.
5　저희 외할머니가 서울에 계세요.
6　저희 외삼촌이 뉴욕에 계세요.
7　우리 형이 대학원생이에요.
8　우리 손자가 한국에 있어요.

UNIT 9
Numbers, ordinals, and plural marker 들 *tŭl*

Sino-Korean numbers and native Korean numbers

In Korean, there are two parallel sets of numbers. One of these was borrowed from Chinese long ago and is now part of the Korean number system. The numbers belonging to this set are called Sino-Korean numbers. The other set is of native origin. The numbers belonging to this set are called native Korean numbers. These two sets are shown below.

Arabic		Korean numbers Sino-Korean	Native Korean
	0	영/공	–
	1	일	하나 (한)*
	2	이	둘 (두)*
	3	삼	셋 (세)*
	4	사	넷 (네)*
	5	오	다섯
	6	육	여섯
	7	칠	일곱
	8	팔	여덟
	9	구	아홉
	10	십	열
	11	십일	열하나
	12	십이	열둘
	13	십삼	열셋
	14	십사	열넷
	15	십오	열다섯
	16	십육	열여섯
	17	십칠	열일곱
	18	십팔	열여덟
	19	십구	열아홉
	20	이십	스물 (스무)*

30	삼십	서른
40	사십	마흔
50	오십	쉰
60	육십	예순
70	칠십	일흔
80	팔십	여든
90	구십	아흔
100	백	–
1,000	천	–
10,000	만	–
100,000	십만	–
1,000,000	백만	–
10,000,000	천만	–
100,000,000	억	–

As seen above, the Korean number system is more systematic than the English number system when it comes to the formation of higher numbers. For instance, while English uses special words for 11 through 19, such as eleven, twelve and so on, Korean numbers are formed "ten + one" (십일) or (열하나), "ten + two" (십이) or (열둘) and so on.

For multiples of ten, Sino-Korean numbers are simple combinations: 20 is "two + ten" (이십), 30 is "three + ten" (삼십), and so on. However, native Korean numbers have special words, as 20 is 스물, 30 is 서른, and so on. In addition, the native Korean number set does not have the number "zero."

The use of Sino-Korean numbers and native Korean numbers differs in a number of ways. First, as indicated by the asterisk mark above, native Korean numbers "one," "two," "three," "four," and "twenty" have slightly modified forms. Koreans use these modified forms when they count one of these native numbers with a counter (e.g., 명 a counter for person). For instance, one person would be 한 명, rather than 하나 명.

Second, Koreans use native Korean numbers when counting a small number of objects. For instance, three bottles of beers would be 맥주 세병 (beer + three + bottles). However, when counting a large number of objects, they prefer using Sino-Korean numbers, as "62 bottles of beers" would be 맥주 육십이 병.

Third, from 100 and above, Koreans use only Sino-Korean numbers. Consequently, 134 would be read as 백삼십사. It is optional to add 일 to the number that starts with 1, such as 100, 1000, and so on, however, it is more common to say the number without it. For instance, for 100, saying "백 (hundred)" is more common than saying "일백 (one hundred)."

125	백이십오
247	이백사십칠

539	오백삼십구
764	칠백육십사
1,457	천사백오십칠
83,625	팔만 삼천육백이십오

It is rare but you can read a number that is over 100, by combining a Sino-Korean number and a native Korean number. For instance, 134 can be read as 백서른 넷 (Sino-Korean number + native Korean number). However, the use of Sino-Korean numbers is more dominant than a mixed use of both sets of numbers.

Finally, Koreans in general use Sino-Korean numbers when doing mathematical calculations.

$8 \times 3 = 24$	팔 곱하기 삼은 이십사
$12 + 7 = 19$	십이 더하기 칠은 십구
$9 - 4 = 5$	구 빼기 사는 오
$20 \div 5 = 4$	이십 나누기 오는 사

Counting

There are two ways of counting countable objects. You can just use a number by itself or use a number with a counter (the function of a counter is to indicate the type of noun being counted). When counting without a counter, you use native Korean numbers. For instance, for "two students," you can say 학생 둘 (noun + number).

One student	학생 하나
Two students	학생 둘
Three students	학생 셋
Four students	학생 넷
Five students	학생 다섯
Six students	학생 여섯
Ten students	학생 열

Counting items with a counter can take the following structure: "noun (being counted) + number + counter." Consequently, for "five students" you would say "학생 + 다섯 + 명."

When you use native Korean numbers with a counter, you should remember that native Korean numbers for 1, 2, 3, 4, and 20 have slightly different forms: 하나/한, 둘/두, 셋/세, 넷/네, and 스물/스무. Consequently, one student would be "학생 한 명" rather than "학생 하나 명," twenty students would be "학생 스무 명" rather than "학생 스물 명."

1 Korean person	한국인 한 명	
2 Korean people	한국인 두 명	
3 Korean people	한국인 세 명	
4 Korean people	한국인 네 명	
5 Korean people	한국인 다섯 명	
6 Korean people	한국인 여섯 명	
14 Korean people	한국인 열네 명	
15 Korean people	한국인 열다섯 명	
20 Korean people	한국인 스무 명	(or 한국인 이십 명)
21 Korean people	한국인 스물 한 명	(or 한국인 이십일 명)
32 Korean people	한국인 서른 두 명	(or 한국인 삼십이 명)
43 Korean people	한국인 마흔 세 명	(or 한국인 사십세 명)
54 Korean people	한국인 쉰 네 명	(or 한국인 오십사 명)
65 Korean people	한국인 예순 다섯 명	(or 한국인 육십오 명)
76 Korean people	한국인 일흔 여섯 명	(or 한국인 칠십육 명)
87 Korean people	한국인 여든 일곱 명	(or 한국인 팔십칠 명)
98 Korean people	한국인 아흔 여덟 명	(or 한국인 구십팔 명)
107 Korean people	한국인 백일곱 명	(or 한국인 백칠 명)
145 Korean people	한국인 백마흔 다섯 명	(or 한국인 백사십오 명)

Notice that that there is no change in 스물 when it is combined with a number, as in "학생 스물 한 명" (21 students). In addition, when the number is large (e.g., above twenty), Sino-Korean numbers can be used as well.

Ordinals

The Sino-Korean and native Korean numbers differ in the formation of ordinals (e.g., regarding order, rank or position in a series). For Sino-Korean numbers, Koreans attach the prefix 제 to a number. For instance, "the first" is 제 일, "the eleventh" is 제 십일, and so on. For native Korean numbers, they add 번째 to a number. Accordingly, "the fifth" is 다섯 번째, "the eleventh" is 열한 번째, and so on. The only exception is that 하나 "the native number for one" is not used for the ordinal, but one needs to use the special word, 첫, as 첫 번째, not 한 번째.

The first	제 일	첫 번째
The second	제 이	두 번째
The third	제 삼	세 번째
The fourth	제 사	네 번째
The fifth	제 오	다섯 번째
The tenth	제 십	열 번째
The sixteenth	제 십육	열여섯 번째
The twentieth	제 이십	스무 번째
The thirty-sixth	제 삼십 육	서른 여섯 번째

Plural marker 들

You probably wonder by now whether Koreans care whether a noun is singular or plural. It is because none of the examples above carry any plural marker. The plural marker for Korean is 들. However, its usage differs from that of English, such as the plural "s." English is very specific with respect to number in that when there is more than one item, the item must be marked by the plural "s." However, Korean nouns are not specific about the number. In other words, the Korean language does not have a grammatical category of number.

For instance, "one student" in Korean is 한 학생 and "five students" is 다섯 학생. Notice that the noun 학생 "student" does not undergo any change in form. Consider the following sentence 의자하고 책상이 있어요. The translation of this sentence can be fourfold, as shown.

I have a chair and a desk.
I have some chairs and a desk.
I have a chair and some desks.
I have some chairs and some desks.

You may wonder then when 들 is used. Koreans optionally add 들 to the noun when they want to emphasize the plurality of the nouns they are referring to. For instance, 학생이 와요 may mean "a student comes" and also mean "some students come." However, Koreans can optionally add 들 as 학생들이 와요 "students come," if they wish to emphasize the plurality of 학생.

Koreans use 들 for other cases too, such as adding the marker not only to the noun but also to pronouns. For instance, although it may sound redundant, Koreans can add 들 to 우리 "we," as in 우리들 "we." Notice that 우리 is already plural. Again, such usage is for adding emphasis.

Exercises

Exercise 9.1

Express the following Sino-Korean numbers in figures:

1 십팔	6 십칠	11 이십사
2 구	7 육십삼	12 구십이
3 사십일	8 칠십오	13 이백삼십
4 팔십일	9 오십육	14 육백칠
5 천사백오십구	10 백이	15 만 팔천칠백사십육

Exercise 9.2

Express the following native Korean numbers in figures:

1	일곱	6	스물 셋	11	아흔
2	열여덟	7	서른 셋	12	일흔 둘
3	스물 다섯	8	열하나	13	마흔 여덟
4	열일곱	9	예순 넷	14	쉰 여섯
5	여든 일곱	10	마흔 아홉	15	스물 둘

Exercise 9.3

Write the following numbers in native Korean numbers:

1	3	6	18	11	32
2	16	7	20	12	87
3	45	8	52	13	19
4	92	9	30	14	24
5	11	10	63	15	75

Exercise 9.4

Write the following numbers in Sino-Korean numbers:

1	6	6	15	11	29
2	11	7	153	12	18
3	37	8	61	13	372
4	42	9	74	14	99
5	517	10	3021	15	53,276

Exercise 9.5

Translate the following into both Sino-Korean and native Korean numbers:

Example: The first
= 제 일 / 첫 째

1 the eighth
2 the twenty-seventh
3 the second
4 the thirtieth
5 the fortieth
6 the fifteenth
7 the eighty-sixth
8 the twentieth
9 the twenty-fourth
10 the sixteenth

Exercise 9.6

Translate the following into English:

Example: 학생 둘 = two students
             한국인 마흔 여덟 명 = 48 Korean people

1 학생 아홉   6 학생 셋
2 학생 스물 네 명   7 학생 열다섯 명
3 한국인 여덟 명   8 한국인 열여섯 명
4 한국인 서른 두 명   9 한국인 백오십팔 명
5 한국인 천사백오십이 명   10 한국인 팔십구 명

UNIT 10

Counters, question word 몇 *myŏt*, and some time expressions

Counters

What a counter does is to classify nouns according to common attributes for numbering purposes. Therefore, by using a counter, you can provide more information about the object you count. The Korean language has an extensive list of counters. Some counters are used only with the native Korean numbers, whereas some counters are used only with the Sino-Korean numbers. Table 10.1 shows the counters that are normally used with the native Korean numbers. However, when the number is above 20 these counters can also be used with Sino-Korean numbers.

Table 10.1 Some major Korean counters used with native Korean numbers

counter	kinds of things counted	examples of counting
명	persons	한 명, 두 명, 세 명, . . . 열명, . . .
사람	persons	한 사람, 두사람, 세사람, . . . 다섯사람, . . .
마리	animals	한 마리, 두 마리, 세 마리, . . .열네 마리, . . .
쌍	couples (people and animals)	한 쌍, 두 쌍, 세 쌍, . . . 여덟쌍, . . .
송이	flowers	한 송이, 두 송이, 세 송이, . . .열 송이, . . .
다발	bunches (of flowers)	한 다발, 두 다말, 세 다발, . . .열 다발, . . .
그루	trees	한 그루, 두 그루, 세 그루, . . .열네 그루, . . .
조각	slices	한 조각, 두 조각, 세 조각, . . .다섯 조각, . . .
개	items, units	한 개, 두 개 , 세 개, . . . 열 개, . . .
상자	boxes	한 상자, 두 상자, 세 상자, . . . 일곱상자, . . .
대	machines, cars	한 대, 두 대, 세 대, . . .아홉 대, . . .
채	houses, buildings	한 채, 두 채, 세 채, . . .여덟 채, . . .
시	o'clock	한 시, 두 시, 세 시, . . .열 두시, . . .
시간	hours (duration)	한 시간, 두 시간, 세 시간, ...스무 시간, . . .
달	months (duration)	한 달, 두 달, 세 달, . . . 아홉달, . . .
해	years	한 해, 두 해, 세 해, . . .여섯 해, . . .
살	years of age	한 살, 두 살, 세 살, . . .서른 두살, . . .
번	times	한 번, 두 번, 세 번, . . .여섯 번, . . .
잔	cupfuls	한 자, 두 잔, 세 잔, . . .열다섯 잔, . . .

Table 10.1 continued

counter	kinds of things counted	examples of counting
병	bottles	한 병, 두병, 세 병, . . . 여덟 병, . . . 쉰 두 병, . . .
봉지	paper bags	한 봉지, 두 봉지, 세 봉지, . . .스무 봉지, . . .
장	pieces of paper	한 장, 두 장, 세 장, . . . 서른장, . . .
권	books	한 권, 두 권, 세 권, . . .열네 권, . . .
군데	places	한 군데, 두 군데, 세 군데, . . . 일곱군데, . . .
켤레	pairs of shoes	한 켤레, 두 켤레, 세 켤레, . . .열 켤레, . . .
벌	clothes	한 벌, 두 벌, 세 벌, . . . 열벌, . . .
가지	kinds	한 가지, 두 가지, 세 가지, . . . 열다섯가지, . . .

On the other hand, Table 10.2 shows the counters that are used only with Sino-Korean numbers. Notice that when the counter is a loanword, such as 달라 "dollars," 마일 "miles," and 미터 "meters," Koreans in general prefer to use Sino-Korean numbers, as in 십오 달라 "fifteen dollars."

Table 10.2 Some major Korean counters used with Sino-Korean numbers

counter	kinds of things counted	examples of counting
일	days	일 일, 이 일, 삼 일, . . . 사십오일, . . .
월	month names	일 월, 이 월, 삼 월, . . . 팔월, . . .
개월	months (duration)	일 개월, 이 개월, 삼 개월, . . . 칠개월, . . .
년	years	일 년, 이 년, 삼 년, . . . 구년, . . .
분	minutes	일 분, 이 분, 삼 분, . . . 오십육분, . . .
초	seconds	일 초, 이 초, 삼 초, . . . 십칠초, . . .
층	floors (of a building)	일 층, 이 층, 삼 층, . . . 삼십사층, . . .
달라	dollars	일 달라, 이 달라, 삼 달라, . . . 백오십팔 달라, . . .
파운드	pounds (sterling)	일 파운드, 이 파운드, 삼 파운드, . . . 십 파운드, . . .
마일	miles	일 마일, 이 마일, 삼 마일, . . . 칠십구 마일, . . .

As seen above, the choice of a certain counter depends on the kinds of objects. However, one must know what counter is used with either a native Korean number or a Sino-Korean number. For instance, when counting minutes, you have to use 분 after a Sino-Korean number, as in 오 분 "five minutes."

A few counters, such as 주일 or 주간 "week," can be used with both Sino-Korean numbers as well as native Korean numbers. For instance, one week can be either 한 주간 or 일 주간 and five weeks can be either 다섯 주간 or 오 주간. However, the use of Sino-Korean numbers with this counter is more common.

Question word 몇

Korean has a question word 몇 "how many." The word cannot be used on its own but must precede a counter. For example, a specific question expression such as "how many people" would be 몇 명, "how many months" would be 몇 달, and so on. One can form various question expressions using the aforementioned counters, such as:

몇 명? "How many people?"
몇 개? "How many items?"
몇 시? "What time?"
몇 살? "How old?"
몇 병? "How many bottles?"
몇 권? "How many (books)?"
몇 월? "What month?"
몇 층? "What floor?"

Some frequently used counters

Using the appropriate counters with the right number set is a systematic but complex process. Students need to practice them in order to be proficient in using them. For instance, let us elaborate on some of the frequently used counters used for telling times, days, months, and years.

Telling times

Koreans use native Korean numbers for 시 "o'clock" but Sino-Korean numbers for 분 "minutes." In addition, for a.m. and p.m., Koreans use the following five words: 아침 "morning" or 오전 "before noon" for a.m., and 오후 "afternoon," 저녁 "evening," and 밤 "night" for p.m., at the beginning of the expression.

07:36 a.m.	아침 (or 오전) 일곱 시 삼십육 분
08:10 a.m.	아침 (or 오전) 여덟 시 십 분
10:45 a.m.	오전 열 시 사십오 분
02:50 p.m.	오후 두 시 오십 분
06:17 p.m.	저녁 (or 오후) 여섯 시 십칠 분
09:24 p.m.	밤 (or 오후) 아홉 시 이십사 분
11:38 p.m.	밤 (or 오후) 열한 시 삼십팔 분

To say half past, you can either say "삼십 분" or an expression 반, meaning "a half." Consequently, the Korean expression for telling 11:30 p.m. can be: 오후 (or 밤) 열 한시 삼십 분 (or 반).

Counting days

Counting days with Sino-Korean numbers is regular. You need to add 일 "a counter for day" after the number, such as 일 일, 이 일, 삼 일, and so on. However, counting days with native Korean numbers is irregular, in that there are special words for days up to 20 as shown below.

one day	일 일	하루
two days	이 일	이틀
three days	삼 일	사흘
four days	사 일	나흘
five days	오 일	닷새
six days	육 일	엿새
seven days	칠 일	이레
eight days	팔 일	여드레
nine days	구 일	아흐레
ten days	십 일	열흘
eleven days	십일 일	열하루
twelve days	십이 일	열이틀
thirteen days	십삼 일	열사흘
twenty days	이십 일	스무날

After 20, only Sino-Korean expressions are used.

Counting months and years

Koreans use Sino-Korean numbers for counting months. Hence, you need to add 월 "months" after a Sino-Korean number, as in 일 월, 이 월, 삼 월, and so on. However, be careful that Koreans do not say June as 육월 but 유월 and October not as 십월 but 시월.

January	일 월
February	이 월
March	삼 월
April	사 월
May	오 월
June	유 월
July	칠 월
August	팔 월
September	구 월
October	시 월
November	십일 월
December	십이 월

For months (duration), however, you can use either native Korean numbers or Sino-Korean numbers. When counting with Sino-Korean numbers, you add 개월 after the number as in 일 개월, 이 개월, 삼 개월, and so on. When counting with native Korean numbers, you add 달 after the number, as in 한 달, 두 달, and so on.

1 month (duration)	일 개월	한 달
2 months	이 개월	두 달
3 months	삼 개월	세 달 (or 석 달)
4 months	사 개월	네 달 (or 넉 달)
5 months	오 개월	다섯 달
6 months	육 개월	여섯 달
7 months	칠 개월	일곱 달
8 months	팔 개월	여덟 달
9 months	구 개월	아홉 달

For years, Koreans normally use Sino-Korean numbers with 년 "year," such as 일 년, 이 년, 삼 년, and so on. They use native Korean numbers for years only for small numbers, such as 한 해 and 두 해. However, Koreans rarely use native Korean numbers beyond 두 해.

1 year	일 년	한 해
2 years	이 년	두 해
3 years	삼 년	–
4 years	사 년	–
5 years	오 년	–
60 years	육십 년	–
100 years	백 년	–

Dates

Let us put all these expressions together. Koreans give dates starting from the largest unit to the smallest. This is the opposite of the English expression. For instance, date information such as "2:19 p.m., 18 May, 1970" is said as "(일)천구백 칠십년 오월 십팔일, 오후 두 시 십구 분." Here are more examples:

9:35 a.m., 11 April, 2004
이천사 년, 사 월 십일 일, 오전 아홉 시 삼십오 분

3:57 p.m., 25 December, 1992
(일)천구백 구십이 년, 십이 월 이십오 일, 오후 세 시 오십칠 분

7:08 a.m., 16 March, 1979
(일)천구백 칠십구 년, 삼 월 십육 일, 오전 일곱 시 팔 분

Exercises

Exercise 10.1

Translate the following into English:

Example: 두 명
= two people

1 세 마리	6 다섯 조각	11 열 번
2 네 시간	7 여섯 병	12 칠십육 마일
3 한 가지	8 스무살	13 삼백오십구 달라
4 열 세개	9 스물네 권	14 십팔 개월
5 서른 여섯 쌍	10 아흔 여덟 명	15 백이십 분

Exercise 10.2

Translate the following into Korean:

Korean: five people
= 다섯 명

1 7 bottles	6 2 places	11 3 couples
2 9 slices	7 12 boxes	12 1 paper bag
3 11 years old	8 8 cups	13 September
4 4 floors	9 13 months	14 60 seconds
5 36 years	10 6 items	15 5 hours

Exercise 10.3

Translate the following into figures:

Example: 오후 세 시 오십육 분
= 03:56 p.m.

1 오전 열 시 사십오 분	6 오전 아홉 시 삼십이 분
2 오후 일곱 시 오십 분	7 오후 여섯 시 십팔 분
3 아침 여덟 시	8 아침 열 시 구 분
4 저녁 여섯 시 이십칠 분	9 저녁 일곱 시 반
5 오전 네 시 사십육 분	10 오후 다섯 시 삼십사 분

Exercise 10.4

Write the following times in Korean:

Example: 09:27 p.m.
        = 오후 아홉 시 이십칠 분

1 11:15 p.m.   6 08:06 a.m.
2 10:32 p.m.   7 06:23 a.m.
3 11:25 a.m.   8 06:28 p.m.
4 02:30 p.m.   9 04:09 p.m.
5 03:48 a.m.   10 05:51 a.m.

Exercise 10.5

Write the following dates in Korean:

Example: 15 August, 1945
        = (일)천구백사십오 년, 팔 월, 십오 일

1 16 March, 1943
2 18 January, 1972
3 25 December, 1965
4 14 February, 1959
5 7 May, 1970
6 31 September, 1994
7   4 July, 2001
8   5 November, 2006
9 30 April, 1936
10 12 August, 1998

Exercise 10.6

Translate the following into English:

Example: 고양이 [cats] 다섯 마리
        = five cats

1 중국인 [Chinese people] 네 명   6 호랑이 [tiger] 세 마리
2 물 [water] 다섯 잔   7 자전거 [bikes] 열한 대
3 집 [house] 여덟 채   8 소설책 [novel] 아홉 권
4 운동화 [sneakers] 두 켤레   9 장미 [rose] 여섯 송이
5 피자 [pizza] 열 조각   10 포도주 [wine] 열두 병

Exercise 10.7

Translate the following into Korean:

Example: Five cats [고양이]
           = 고양이 다섯 마리

1 7 Americans [미국인]
2 5 roses [장미]
3 10 Korean books [한국어 책]
4 3 cars [자동차]
5 6 trees [나무]

6 2 pairs of shoes [신발]
7 8 cups of coffee [커피]
8 9 bottles of beers [맥주]
9 4 Japanese [일본인]
10 20 dogs [개]

UNIT 11

The copula 이다/아니다 and the verb of existence and location 있다/없다

In English, copulas "am," "are," and/or "is" can express at least two things. First, they are used to indicate the equational expression (e.g., something equals something), as in "John <u>is</u> a student" or "Hyundai <u>is</u> an automobile company." In addition, they indicate that something is located or existing as in "There <u>are</u> Korean people" or "Honolulu <u>is</u> in Hawaii." In Korean, two different words express these two functions. For the equational expression, Korean has the copula 이다 (or 아니다 for negation). For the verb of existence or location, Korean has the verb 있다 (or 없다 for negation).

Equational expressions 이에요/예요

The dictionary form for the Korean copula is 이다. The stem of the copula is 이 (as you take 다 "the dictionary ending" out). With the polite speech level ending, the copula 이다 becomes 이에요 for the preceding noun that ends in a consonant, as in 데니엘이에요 "(I) am Daniel." For the preceding noun that ends in a vowel, the copula 이다 becomes 예요, as in 앤드류예요 "(I) am Andrew." With different speech levels, such as the deferential speech level ending, the copula becomes 입니다 (이 + ㅂ니다).

이에요/예요 always follows the noun it expresses. In other words, it cannot be used separately from the noun. For instance, consider the following sentences:

캐티는 선생님<u>이에요</u> "As for Cathy, (she) is a teacher"
데니엘은 의사<u>예요</u> "As for Daniel, (he) is a medical doctor"

Notice that 이에요 attaches to 선생님 (since the last syllable 님 ends in a consonant ㅁ), while in the second sentence, 예요 comes after 의사 (as the last syllable 사 ends in the vowel ㅏ).

Negation - 이/가 아니에요

The Korean copula for negation is 아니다. The stem of the negative copula 아니 becomes 아니에요 with the polite speech level ending. For negating an equational expression, the subject particle 이/가 is used with 아니에요, as in:

니콜은 한국사람<u>이 아니에요</u> "As for Nicole, (she) is not a Korean"
매튜는 엔지니어<u>가 아니에요</u> "As for Matthew, (he) is not an engineer"

Notice that the noun that is being negated has the subject particle 이 (after the noun ending in a consonant) or 가 (after the noun endings in a vowel).

Existence and location with 있어요/ 없어요 and case particle 에

The Korean verb 있다 means "exist/exists" or "there is/are." For negation, Korean has a separate verb 없다 "do/does not exist" or "is/are not located." Since 있다 expresses "something exists" or "something is located (somewhere)," it is normally called the verb of existence and location.

When referring to a location of an object, you need a location, a locative particle "에," and the verb of existence and location "있어요." For instance, consider the following sentences.

존이 런던에 있어요 "John is in London"
호놀룰루가 하와이에 있어요 "Honolulu is in Hawaii"

Notice that the locations (런던, 하와이) are marked by the particle 에, and they are followed by the verb 있어요.

For a more specific location reference, various Korean location nouns¯ can be used. Korean has the following location nouns:

위	"above"
아래	"below"
밑	"under"
뒤	"behind"
앞	"front"
안	"inside"
밖	"outside"
옆	"side"
오른쪽	"right side"
왼쪽	"left side"

Using one of the location nouns, you can be more explicit in referring to the location and/or position of the noun, as in 책이 책상 <u>위에</u> 있어요 "The book is on the table."

You may wonder if these location words are like various prepositions in English such as "above," "below," "on," "beside," and "behind." These English prepositions are similar to Korean location nouns in the sense that they both function to indicate the specific reference of the location. However, they are different in two aspects. First, while English prepositions always appear before the object of the location (as in "above the table"), those in Korean always appear after the object (as in 책상 위 "table-above"). Another difference is that these Korean postpostional elements are nouns and they are normally followed by the locative particle 에, whereas English prepositional elements are not nouns.

있다 vs. 이다

When asking for the specific location of a certain object, Koreans use the question word 어디 "where" with the verb 있다, as in:

은행이 어디(에) 있어요? "Where is the bank (lit., where does the bank exist)?"

Notice that the question word 어디 appears right before the verb 있어요.

One can use 이에요 with 어디, as in 은행이 어디예요? "Where is the bank?" However, notice that the question does not seek the specific location of 은행, rather it simply questions the general whereabouts of 은행. In other words, the copula 이에요 cannot be used to refer to the location of an object.

For example, for the above question, a response such as 은행이 학교 도서관 뒤에 있어요 "The bank is (lit., exists) behind the school library" is acceptable. However, 은행이 학교 도서관 뒤예요 "The bank is the back of the school library" is not acceptable since these two responses do not mean the same thing.

For another example, take the following two sentences:

서울이 한국에 있어요 (O) "Seoul is in Korea (lit., Seoul exists in Korea)"
서울이 한국이에요 (X) "Seoul is Korea"

As seen above, these two sentences do not have the same meaning.

The use of 있다/없다 to express "possession"

Another meaning of 있다/없다 is to express one's possession. In the following example, 있다/없다 is better translated as "have/has."

피터는 애플 컴퓨터(가) <u>있어요</u> "As for Peter, (he) has an Apple Computer"

The literal translation of the above sentence may be "As for Peter, there is an Apple Computer" or "As for Peter, an Apple Computer exists." However, it actually means (or is better translated into English) "As for Peter, (he) has an Apple Computer." Notice that Apple Computer is marked by the subject particle 이/가. KFL learners, whose native language is English, tend to make an error using 을/를 the object particle (instead of 이/가). This is because of the native language transfer effect. They intuitively judge the verb "have" should have an object, since its direct English translation may be "Peter has an Apple Computer."

Exercises

Key vocabulary for Unit 11 exercises

가방 bag
간호사 nurse
개 dog
경찰 police
계산기 calculator
고양이 cat
과학자 scientist
그림 painting
기자 journalist
꽃 flower
대학생 college student
디자이너 designer
모자 hat
볼펜 ball-point pen
빵 bread

사업가 businessman
선생님 teacher
신문 newspaper
엔지니어 engineer
열쇠 key

외교관 diplomat
우산 umbrella
의사 medical doctor
의자 chair
자동자 car
자전거 bike
책 book
책상 desk
침대 bed
컴퓨터 computer
회계사 accountant
휴지통 waste basket

Exercise 11.1

Look at the following list and to the given name add 예요/이에요, as in the example. Then translate the sentence.

> Example: 뉴욕
> = 뉴욕이에요 "(It) is New York"

1 서울
2 토쿄
3 베이징
4 로마
5 카이로
6 런던
7 와싱턴
8 뱅쿠버
9 상파울로
10 베를린

Exercise 11.2

Look at the following list and make sentences using (이/가) 아니에요, as in the example.

> Example: 수잔 ≠ 선생님
> = 수잔은 선생님이 아니에요

1 바바라 ≠ 의사   _____
2 리처드 ≠ 대학생   _____

```
 3  에릭 ≠ 디자이너      _____
 4  씬디 ≠ 경찰          _____
 5  이사벨 ≠ 기자         _____
 6  데니엘 ≠ 외교관       _____
 7  조지 ≠ 회계사        _____
 8  사이몬 ≠ 과학자       _____
 9  에비게일 ≠ 사업가     _____
10  다이에나 ≠ 간호사     _____
```

Exercise 11.3

Translate the following sentences into Korean.

Example: "As for Cindy, (she) is a scientist"   = 씬디는 과학자예요
          "As for Danny, (he) is not a scientist"   = 데니는 과학자가
                                                       아니에요

 1 "As for John, (he) is a teacher."
 2 "As for Sandra, (she) is not a teacher."
 3 "As for Peter, (he) is a medical doctor."
 4 "As for Mary, (she) is not a medical doctor."
 5 "As for Lisa, (she) is an engineer."
 6 "As for Steve, (he) is not an engineer."
 7 "As for Ben, (he) is a nurse."
 8 "As for Linda, (she) is not a nurse."
 9 "As for Nancy, (she) is a college student."
10 "As for Charles, (he) is not a college student."

Exercise 11.4

Complete each sentence as shown in the example.

  Example: (오페라 하우스) (시드니)
            = 오페라 하우스가 시드니에 있어요

 1 (차이나타운) (샌프란시스코)
 2 (바티칸) (이탈리아)
 3 (상하이) (중국)
 4 (그랜드캐넌) (아리조나)
 5 (디지니월드) (플로리다)
 6 (피라미드) (이집트)
 7 (아마존) (브라질)

8 (에베레스트산) (네팔)
9 (에펠타워) (파리)
10 (할리우드) (캘리포니아)

Exercise 11.5

Translate the following Korean sentences into English.

> Example: 브래드는 기타가 있어요.
>   = "As for Brad, (he) has a bicycle."

1 마리아는 클래식 기타가 있어요.
2 애니는 키보드가 있어요.
3 제임스는 베이스 기타가 있어요.
4 폴은 드럼이 있어요.
5 엘리샤는 바이올린이 있어요.
6 에릭은 섹스폰이 있어요.
7 로버트는 클라리넷이 있어요.
8 케빈은 트럼펫이 있어요.
9 리사는 피아노가 있어요.
10 조앤은 첼로가 있어요.

Exercise 11.6

Translate the following sentences into Korean.

> Example: "As for Brad, (he) has a bag"
>   = 브래드는 가방이 있어요

1 "As for Jerry, (he) has money."
2 "As for Barbara, (she) has the key."
3 "As for Justin, (he) has the painting."
4 "As for Gabriel, (he) has the flower."
5 "As for Adam, (he) has the hat."
6 "As for Lisa, (she) has the bread."
7 "As for William, (he) has a cat."
8 "As for Harry, (he) has the umbrella."
9 "As for Hugh, (he) has a newspaper."
10 "As for Diane, (she) has a car."
11 "As for George, (he) has a bike."
12 "As for Naomi, (she) has a dog."

Exercise 11.7

Fill in the blank with an appropriate location word.

    Example: 우산은 책상 _____ (below) 에 있어요
            = 밑

1 책은 책상 _____ (above) 에 있어요.
2 휴지통은 책상 _____ (behind) 에 있어요.
3 가방은 책상 _____ (below) 에 있어요.
4 침대는 책상 _____ (side) 에 있어요.
5 의자는 책상 _____ (front) 에 있어요.
6 볼펜은 책상 _____ (inside) 에 있어요.
7 계산기는 책상 _____ (left side) 에 있어요.
8 컴퓨터는 책상 _____ (right side) 에 있어요.

UNIT 12

Case particles 1
을 *ŭl*/를 *lŭl* and (으)로 *(ŭ)ro*

The direct object particle 을/를

The direct object refers to a noun that experiences the action indicated by the verb. In English the direct object of the sentence is typically determined by the place where it appears. For instance, the direct object of the sentence "I eat steak" is "steak," as the word "steak" appears after the verb "eat." In Korean, however the direct object is primarily determined by the direct object particle 을/를. Just like the subject particle, the direct object particle 을/를 is a two-form case particle: 을 is used when the preceding noun ends in a consonant, and 를 is used when the preceding noun ends in a vowel.

책을 읽어요 "(I) read a book"
연필을 사요 "(I) buy a pencil"
영화를 봐요 "(I) see a movie"
콜라를 마셔요 "(I) drink cola"

Although the particle 을/를 typically marks the direct object of the transitive verb in Korean, there is one exceptional case where it can appear with the intransitive verb, such as 가다 "go" or 오다 "come." Consider the following sentences:

앤드류는 오전 8시에 학교에 가요 "As for Andrew, (he) goes to school at 8 a.m."
앤드류는 오전 8시에 학교를 가요 "As for Andrew, (he) goes to school at 8 a.m."

Notice that 학교 "school" can be marked by the locative particle "에" as well as the direct object particle "를."

Noun + 을/를 해요

In Korean, one of the most useful ways to change a noun into a verb form is by adding 을/를 해요 to a noun. The verb 하다 "do" is very resourceful and adaptable in that it can come after a noun and transforms the meaning denoted by the noun as the verb form. For instance, consider the following sentences:

> 스티븐이 사인을 해요 "Steven signs" (lit., "does signing")
> 나오꼬가 영어를 잘 해요 "Naoko speaks English well"
> 메리가 축구를 해요 "Mary plays soccer"
> 나탈리가 에어로빅을 해요 "Natalie does aerobics"
> 폴이 서핑을 해요 "Paul surfs"
> 어디서 일을 하세요? "Where do (you) work?"
> 토요일에 제 방 청소를 해요 "(I) clean my room on Saturday"
> 친구 집에서 빨래를 해요 "(I) do laundry at friend's house"
> 학교에서 숙제를 해요 "(I) do homework at school"

In this <u>noun + 을/를 + 해요</u> construction, the noun being used is treated as an independent noun due to the presence of the direct object particle 을/를. However, without the particle, the construction is treated as a compound verb. For instance, the following two sentences have the same meanings:

> 사인을 해요 "(I) do signing"
> 사인해요 "I sign"

Notice that the first sentence has the particle 을, while the second sentence does not have it. There is no difference in their meanings.

In Korean, a sentence may have two object particles. For instance, a sentence "John signs the contract" can be said 존이 계약서를 사인을 해요. However, the same can be said in the following three more ways:

> 존이 계약서 사인해요 "John signs the contract"
> 존이 계약서를 사인해요 "John signs the contract"
> 존이 계약서 사인을 해요 "John signs the contract"

The absence of the particles in the above examples is due to the particle omission tendency in the Korean language.

Case particle (으)로

The case particle (으)로 is a two-form particle: 으로 appears after a noun that ends in a consonant (as in 책<u>으로</u> "by books"); 로 appears after a noun that ends in a vowel (as in 버스<u>로</u> "by bus") or the consonant ㄹ

(as in 신발로 "by shoes"). The particle (으) 로 can express the following five things: (1) means, (2) direction, (3) selection, (4) the change of state, and (5) reason.

Means

First, the particle (으)로 indicates that the noun it attaches to is a tool or an instrument. It is translated in English as "by means of" or "with."

펜으로 사인하세요 "Please sign with a pen"
학교에 버스로 가요 "(I) go to school by bus"
공항에 택시로 가세요 "Go to the airport by taxi"
와인은 포도로 만들어요 "As for wine, (one) makes it with grape"
김치는 배추로 만들어요 "As for kimchi, (one) makes it with cabbage"

Direction

Second, the particle indicates the direction "to" or "toward." In the previous section however, it was noted that the direction (e.g., destination) can be marked by the case particle 에. The difference between 에 and (으)로 is that while 에 indicates a specific location or destination, (으) 로 indicates a more general direction of the target location, as in the following sentences:

어디에 가세요? "Where do (you) go?"
어디로 가세요? "In what direction, do (you) go?"

Here are some more examples:

왼쪽으로 가세요 "Go toward the left side"
소파는 TV쪽으로 움직여 주세요 "Please move the sofa toward the TV side"
앞으로 달리세요 "Run toward the front"
학교 쪽으로 오세요 "Come in the direction of the school"
커피숍 쪽으로 나가세요 "Go out in the direction of the coffee shop"

Selection

Third, the particle indicates that the preceding noun is a selection from several options. For instance, consider the following sentences.

Salesman: 무슨 사이즈로 드릴까요? "In what size shall (I) give (it to you)?"
Customer: 스몰로 주세요. "Give (me) the small."

Notice that by using 으로, the salesman implies that there are more than one size. Here are some more examples:

Server: 디저트는 뭘로 하시겠어요? "As for desert, what would (you) like?"
Customer 1:   저는 바닐라 아이스크림으로 주세요. "As for me, give (me) the vanilla ice cream."
Customer 2:   저는 치즈 케이크로 주세요. "As for me, give (me) the cheese cake."

The change of state

Fourth, the particle indicates "the change of state." For instance, consider the following sentences:

피터가 회장으로 선출됐다 "Peter was elected as the president"
삼성이 큰 회사로 성장했다 "Samsung grew up into a big company"
물이 얼음으로 변했다 "Water changed into ice"

Notice that in the examples above, the particle (으)로 marks the result of the change.

Reasons

Fifth, the particle indicates "the reason." Consider the following examples.

우리는 학교 야구 팀의 승리로 기뻐했어요 "As for us, (we) rejoiced because of the school baseball team's victory"
차 사고로 다리를 다쳤어요 "(I) got hurt in the leg due to the car accident"
서울이 1988 올림픽으로 유명해 졌어요 "Seoul became well known due to the 1988 Olympics"
이집트가 피라미드로 유명해요 "Egypt is well known because of the Pyramids"

Exercises

Key vocabulary for Unit 12 exercises

과일 fruit
게임 game
공부하다 to study
국수 noodle

기숙사 dormitory
꽃 flower
담배 cigarette
도서관 library
마시다 to drink
만나다 to meet
먹다 to eat
문 door
문화 culture
물 water

바꿔주다 to change
배우다 to learn
보다 to watch
볼펜 ball-point pen
비행기 airplane
빨래 laundry
빵 bread
사다 to buy
사진 picture
산책 stroll
색 color
설거지 dish washing
세수 face washing
손 hand
숙제 homework
쓰다 to write
씻다 to wash

앉다 to sit
약속 promise
얼굴 face
열다 to open
열쇠 key
영화 movie
오른쪽 the right side
외식 eating out
외우다 to memorize
요리 cooking
운동 sports
음악 music
이기다 to win
이름 name
이야기 talking
읽다 to read

자전거 bike
전화 telephone
젓가락 chopsticks
주다 to give
지키다 to keep
찍다 to take (a photograph)
차 car
창문 window
책 book
친구 friend
청소 cleaning
토요일 Saturday
파랑 blue (color)
팔다 to sell
피우다 to smoke
하얀색 white color
흔들다 to shake

Exercise 12.1

Using the <u>Noun + 을/를 + 해요</u> pattern, complete the sentence with appropriate noun and write the meaning.

Example: 노래
= 노래를 해요 "(I) sing a song (lit., do a song)"

1 빨래
2 외식
3 설거지
4 요리
5 세수
6 이야기
7 산책
8 청소
9 전화
10 숙제

Exercise 12.2

Translate the following into Korean.

Example: "(I) jog everyday"
= 매일 조깅을 해요

1 "(I) do aerobics everyday."
2 "(I) take a shower everyday."
3 "(I) do homework everyday."
4 "(I) shop (lit. do shopping) everyday."
5 "(I) practice (lit. do) yoga everyday."
6 "(I) make (lit. do) a phone call everyday."

Exercise 12.3

Answer the following questions in Korean using the cues.

> Example: 무슨 음식을 좋아하세요? (한국 음식)
> "What kind of food do (you) like?"
> = 한국 음식을 좋아해요

1 무슨 음악을 좋아하세요? (재즈) "What kind of music do (you) like?"
2 무슨 운동을 좋아하세요? (조깅) "What kind of sport do (you) like?"
3 무슨 영화를 좋아하세요? (코미디) "What kind of movie do (you) like?"
4 무슨 과일을 좋아하세요? (오렌지) "What kind of fruit do (you) like?"
5 무슨 색을 좋아하세요? (파랑색) "What kind of color do (you) like?"
6 무슨 꽃을 좋아하세요? (튤립) "What kind of flower do (you) like?"
7 무슨 차를 좋아하세요? (SUV) "What kind of car do (you) like?"

Exercise 12.4

Translate the following into English.

> Example: 창문을 열어요
> = "(I) open a window"

1 이름을 외워요.
2 게임을 이겨요.
3 책을 읽어요.
4 약속을 지켜요.
5 꽃에 물을 주어요.
6 사진을 찍어요.
7 열쇠를 찾아요.
8 자전거를 팔아요.
9 담배를 피워요.
10 손을 흔들어요.

Exercise 12.5

Translate the following sentences into Korean.

> Example: "Tony does homework"
> = 토니가 숙제를 해요

1 "Peter reads a book at the library."
2 "John washes his face."
3 "Angie drinks coffee at Starbucks."
4 "Matthew watches TV at the dormitory."
5 "William eats bread."
6 "Hillary meets friends."
7 "George buys flowers."
8 "Chris learns Korean."
9 "Catherine writes an e-mail."
10 "Isabel studies Korean culture."

Exercise 12.6

Fill in the blanks with either 로 or 으로:

> Example: 앞 ____오세요 "Please come forward"
> = 으로

Means

1 펜____이름을 쓰세요. "Please write (your) name with a pen."
2 "Happiness" 가 한국어____ "행복"이에요. "Happiness is 'haengbok' in Korean."
3 집에 버스____가요. "(I) go home by bus."
4 비누____얼굴을 씻어요. "(I) wash (my) face with soap."
5 밀가루____빵을 만들어요. "(One) makes bread with flour."

Selection

6 저는 콜라____할래요. "As for me, (I) will have Cola."
7 빨간색 옷____할래요. "(I) will have the red dress."

Direction

8 오늘은 커피 숍____가요. "As for today, (we) go to the coffee shop."
9 이번 주말에 어디__ 갈 거예요? "Where will (you) go this weekend?"
10 뒷쪽____가세요. "Go to the rear."

Change of state

11 더 작은 사이즈____바꿔 주세요. "Please change (it) into a smaller size."

12 아침 수업을 오후 수업____ 바꿨어요. "(I) changed the morning class with an afternoon class."

Reason

13 축제____ 모두가 즐거워했다. "Everyone rejoiced because of the festival."

14 크리스마스 쇼핑____ 가게가 바빴어요. "The store was busy due to the Christmas shopping."

Exercise 12.7

Translate the following into English.

Example: 김치는 배추로 만들어요
= "(One) makes kimchi with cabbage"

1 열쇠로 문을 열어요.
2 뉴욕에 비행기로 가요.
3 저는 블랙 커피로 할래요.
4 하얀색 유니폼으로 샀어요.
5 토요일에 보스톤으로 가요.
6 오른쪽으로 앉으세요.
7 파랑색 볼펜으로 바꿔주세요.
8 더 큰 차로 샀어요.
9 국수는 젓가락으로 먹어요.
10 허니문은 라스베가스로 갈 거예요.

UNIT 13

Case particles 2
의 *ŭi*, 에 *e*, 와 *wa*/과 *kwa*, (이)랑 *irang*, and 하고 *hago*

The case particle 의

The case particle 의 indicates the possessor and possession relationship between two nouns, as in 제임스의 방 "James' room." The first noun is typically the possessor (since it is attached by the particle), and the second noun is the possession. The case particle 의 is a one-form particle. It is the same regardless of whether it attaches to a noun that ends in a vowel or a consonant, as in 수잔의 가방 "Susan's bag" and 토니의 지갑 "Tony's wallet."

The first person possessive pronoun 내 (plain form) and 제 (humble form) are combinations of the first person pronouns and the particle:

나 "I (plain)" + 의 = 내 "my (plain)"
저 "I (humble)" + 의 = 제 "my (humble)"

그 것은 나의 (내) 운동화예요 "As for that, (it) is my sneaker"
토마스는 저의 (제) 친구입니다 "As for Thomas, (he) is my friend"

In a similar manner, the question word 누구의 "whose" is the combination of the question word 누구 "who" and the particle 의, as in 이 것은 누구의 편지예요? "As for this, whose letter is (this)?"

As seen above, the function of the particle 의 resembles that of the English suffix -'s. However, there is one clear difference in their usages. English allows the possessor + 's construction, as in "Steven's" or "Andy's." However, Korean does not allow the possessor noun ending with the particle. Consequently, a sentence like 그 컴퓨터는 스티브의예요 "As for that computer, (it) is Steven's" is unacceptable. For this purpose, a bound noun 것 "thing" typically appears after the particle, as in 그 컴퓨터는 스티브의 것이에요 "As for that computer, (it) is Steven's (thing)."

In colloquial and informal usages, the particle 의 can be often omitted. For instance, 수잔 가방 can be used instead of 수잔의 가방 "Susan's bag" and 스티브 것 (or 스티브 거 for a more colloquial usage) can be used instead of 스티브의 것 "Steven's (thing)."

In summary, there are three ways to express a possessor–possession relationship in Korean:

1 noun 의 noun, as in 데니엘의 지갑 "Daniel's wallet."
2 noun noun, as in 데니엘 지갑 "Daniel wallet."
3 noun 것 (or 거), as in 데니엘 거 "Daniel thing."

The particle 에

The case particle 에 is a one-form particle that expresses four things: (1) the static location, (2) the goal of the action (e.g., destination), (3) times, and (4) quantity.

First, the particle 에 marks the static location, corresponding to "in," "at" or "on" in English. The static location refers to the place where something is (being), at or in. For instance, consider the following sentence:

수잔이 집에 있어요 "Susan is at home"

The home 집 is a static location, where Susan is. Here are more examples.

컴퓨터가 도서관에 있어요 "The computer is at the library"
존이 공항에 있어요 "John is at the airport"
책을 책상에 놓아요 "(I) place a book on the desk"
바티칸이 로마에 있어요 "The Vatican is in Rome"
아마존강이 브라질에 있어요 "The Amazon River is in Brazil"

Notice that all the location nouns above (e.g., 도서관, 공항, 책상) are marked by the particle 에, since they are all static locations.

Second, the particle 에 expresses the goal of the action (e.g., inanimate objects or destinations), corresponding to "to" or "at' in English. Consider the following sentences:

은행에 돈을 부쳐주세요 "Please send the money to the bank"
경찰서에 연락했어요 "(I) contacted the police station"
나라에 세금을 냈어요 "(I) paid taxes to the government"
학교에 전화해요 "(I) make a phone call to school"
내일 시카고에 가요 "(I) go to Chicago tomorrow"
한국에 와요 "(They) come to Korea"
비행기가 오늘 JFK 공항에 도착해요 "The plane arrives at JFK airport today"

Notice that the goals of the actions marked by the particle 에 are all inanimate objects (e.g., 은행, 경찰서, 나라, 학교). In addition, when the particle is used with motion verbs like 가다 "go," 오다 "come," and 도착하다 "arrive," the particle indicates a destination (e.g., 시카고, 한국, 공항).

If the goal of the action is animate, the different particles, such as 한테 and 에게, are used.

"(I) make a phone call to Thomas"
토마스한테 전화해요 (O)
토마스에 전화해요 (X)

"(I) gave the book to Peter"
피터한테 책을 주었어요 (O)
피터에 책을 주었어요 (X)

"(I) talked to the friend"
친구한테 이야기했어요 (O)
친구에 이야기했어요 (X)

Third, the particle 에 marks the time noun, corresponding to "at," "in," or "on" in English.

오전 10 시에 TV 를 봐요 "(I) watch TV at 10:00 a.m."
화요일에 만나요 "(Let us) meet on Tuesday"
오후에 바빠요 "(I am) busy in the afternoon"

One should be careful not to use the particle with all time nouns, since certain time nouns, such as 어제 "yesterday," 오늘 "today," and 내일 "tomorrow," do not take the particle 에. Consequently, a sentence like 내일에 스타벅스에서 만나요 "(Let us) meet at Starbucks tomorrow" is unacceptable due to the use of particle 에.

Lastly, the particle 에 is used to mean "for" or "per," as in "per day."

하루에 몇 시간 TV를 보세요? "How many hours do (you) watch TV per day?"
한 상자에 얼마예요? "How much is (it) per box?"
그 와인은 한 병에 얼마예요? "As for that wine, how much is (it) per bottle?"

The particle 와/과, (이)랑, and 하고

The case particles 와/과, (이)랑, and 하고 mean "and." Their primary function is to link nouns together. First, let us discuss the particle 와/과. The particle 와/과 is a two-form particle. 와 is used with the noun that ends in a vowel (e.g., 토마스와 데니엘 "Thomas and Daniel"), and 과 is used with the noun that ends in a consonant (e.g., 데니엘과 토마스 "Daniel and Thomas"). The particle 와/과 tends to be used in formal or written communication.

> 수잔과 토마스가 미국 사람입니다 "Susan and Thomas are Americans"
> 영미와 재호가 한국 사람입니다 "Youngmee and Jaeho are Koreans"
> 제 형과 누나가 보스톤에서 살아요 "My older brother and older sister live in Boston"
> 한국과 일본이 동아시아에 있습니다 "Korea and Japan are in East Asia"
> 마드리드와 바르셀로나가 스페인에 있습니다 "Madrid and Barcelona are in Spain"

The particle (이)랑 tends to be used for more informal and/or colloquial settings. The particle (이)랑 is also a two-form particle. 이랑 is used with a noun that ends in a consonant, and 랑 is used with a noun that ends in a vowel.

> 수잔이랑 토마스가 미국 사람이에요 "Susan and Thomas are Americans"
> 유아랑 영호가 한국 사람이에요 "Yua and Youngho are Koreans"

The particle 하고 is a one-form particle that comes after a noun regardless of whether it ends in a vowel or a consonant. There is no apparent meaning difference between 하고 and the other two particles 와/과 and (이)랑. However, 하고 seems to be less informal than 와/과 but more formal than (이)랑.

> 토마스하고 수잔이 미국 사람이에요 "Thomas and Susan are Americans"
> 재호하고 수미가 한국 사람이에요 "Jaeho and Soomee are Koreans"
> 주소하고 집 전화 번호를 쓰세요 "Write the address and the home phone number"
> 파리하고 런던을 여행할 거예요 "(I) will travel to Paris and London"
> 스테이크하고 와인을 주문했어요 "(I) ordered steak and wine"

When the subject is understood from the context, it can be omitted. In such cases, the noun with 와/과, (이)랑, or 하고 can stand alone, as in (수잔이) 토마스와 커피를 마셔요 "(Susan) drinks coffee with Thomas." Then, the translation of the particles is "with" rather than "and."

Exercises

Key vocabulary for Unit 13 exercises

가게 store
가을 autumn
공항 airport
교실 classroom
교회 church
기름 oil
기숙사 dormitory
남자 man
돈 money
땅 earth
모자 hat
물 water
바다 sea
반지 ring
방 room
병원 hospital
봄 spring
불 fire

사과 apple
사자 lion
사진 picture
산 mountain
시계 watch
아버지 father
약국 pharmacy
여자 woman
열쇠 key
옷 clothes
일본 Japan

자동차 car
자전거 bike
전쟁 war
중국 China
지갑 wallet
집 house
책방 bookstore
친구 friend

캔디 candy
컴퓨터 computer
펜 pen
평화 peace
하늘 sky
호텔 hotel

Exercise 13.1

Translate the following into English:

> Example: 제니퍼의 가방
>   = "Jennifer's bag"

1 스캇의 자동차
2 그레이스의 반지
3 테드의 크레딧 카드
4 린다의 카메라
5 줄리엣 옷
6 에드워드 아버지
7 로버트 지갑
8 잭클린 돈
9 나탈리 거
10 제인 거

Exercise 13.2

Translate the following into Korean:

> Example: "Jennifer's bag"
>   = 제니퍼의 가방

1 "Tom's computer."
2 "Annie's key."
3 "Joan's pen."
4 "Andrew's water."
5 "Romeo's picture."
6 "Ken's room."
7 "Daniel's watch."
8 "Samantha's hat."
9 "Karen's apple."
10 "Diana's bike."

Exercise 13.3

Write a sentence using the cues provided.

> Example: 전화/ 집
>   = 전화가 집에 있어요

1 책상/ 교실
2 지갑 / 차
3 카메라/ 집
4 책 / 학교
5 수잔 / 서울
6 토마스/ 런던
7 에펠타워 / 파리
8 그랜드캐년 / 아리조나
9 할리우드 / 캘리포니아
10 피라미드 / 이집트

Exercise 13.4

Answer the questions in Korean using the cues provided.

> Example: 어디 가세요? (church)
>   = 교회에 가요

1 (library)
2 (classroom)
3 (airport)
4 (friend's home)
5 (church)
6 (book store)
7 (hospital)
8 (candy shop)
9 (pharmacy)
10 (hotel)

Exercise 13.5

Fill in the blank with either 이랑 or 랑.

> Example: 수잔 ＿＿＿데이트해요 "(I) date Susan"
> = 수잔이랑 데이트 해요

1 친구＿＿＿이야기해요. "(I) chat with a friend."
2 사무엘＿＿＿운동 해요. "(I) exercise with Samuel."
3 제니퍼＿＿＿에어로빅 해요. "(I) do aerobics with Jennifer."
4 데니엘 ＿＿＿요리해요. "(I) cook with Daniel."
5 이사벨＿＿＿쇼핑 해요. "(I) do shopping with Isabel."
6 제임스＿＿＿공부해요. "(I) study with James."
7 캐서린＿＿＿전화 해요. "(I) talk to Catherine over the phone."
8 가족＿＿＿외식 해요. "(I) dine out with family."
9 피터＿＿＿청소해요. "(I) clean (the room) with Peter."
10 선생님＿＿＿노래해요. "(I) sing with the teacher."

Exercise 13.6

Connect two sentences using 하고.

> Example: 사탕이 있어요. 초콜릿이 있어요 "There is a candy.
> There is a chocolate"
> = 사탕하고 초콜릿이 있어요

1 커피가 있어요. 녹차가 있어요. "There is coffee. There is green tea."
2 한국 사람이 있어요. 중국 사람이 있어요. "There is a Korean. There is a Chinese."
3 기타가 있어요. 드럼이 있어요. "There is a guitar. There is a drum."
4 악어가 있어요. 하마가 있어요. "There is an alligator. There is a hippo."
5 개가 있어요. 고양이가 있어요. "There is a dog. There is a cat."
6 사과가 있어요. 오렌지가 있어요. "There is an apple. There is an orange."
7 빵이 있어요. 우유가 있어요. "There is bread. There is milk."
8 컴퓨터가 있어요. 프린터가 있어요. "There is a computer. There is a printer."
9 책상이 있어요. 의자가 있어요. "There is a desk. There is a chair."
10 형이 있어요. 누나가 있어요. "There is an older brother. There is an older sister."

Exercise 13.7

Fill in the blanks with either 와 or 과, and translate the phrase into English:

Example: 여름____겨울
           = 여름과 겨울 "Summer and Winter"

 1 중국___일본
 2 봄___ 가을
 3 소프라노___ 알토
 4 사자___ 하이에나
 5 전쟁___ 평화
 6 하늘___ 땅
 7 산___ 바다
 8 불___ 물
 9 남자___ 여자
10 물___ 기름

UNIT 14

Case particles 3
에서 *esŏ*, 에게 *ege*, 한테 *hant'e*, 께 *kke*,
에게서 *egesŏ*, and 한테서 *hant'esŏ*

The particle 에서

The case particle 에서 is a one-form particle and is used to express two
things: (1) the dynamic location, or (2) the source of action. A dynamic
location refers to the place where an action takes place. Consider the
following sentence:

존이 학교 식당에서 점심을 먹어요 "John eats lunch at the school
cafeteria"

Notice that 학교 식당 "the school cafeteria" is a dynamic location, where
the action (e.g., eating lunch) takes place. In fact, the use of the particle
에서 is determined by the type of verb the sentence has. Whenever the
verb denotes an activity such as playing, doing, meeting, working, studying,
and so forth, 에서 must be used. Here are more examples:

앤드류가 학교에서 린다를 만나요 "Andrew meets Susan at school"
(X) 앤드류가 학교에 린다를 만나요 "Andrew meets Susan at school"

In the first sentence above, the particle 에서 is used, since the school is the
dynamic location where the action (e.g., meeting Susan) is taking place.
The use of 에 in this context would be ungrammatical.

Second, the particle 에서 marks a source of action (e.g., starting location),
corresponding to "from" in English. Consider the following examples:

보스톤에서 뉴욕시까지 가요 "(I) go to New York City from Boston"
여기에서 저기까지 청소해 주세요 "Please clean from here to there"
나오꼬가 일본에서 와요 "Naoko comes from Japan"

Notice that the sources of action above are all inanimate entities (e.g.,
places such as Boston, here, and Japan). If the sources of actions are
animate such as persons and animals, different particles such as 한테서 or
에게서 should be used.

The particles 한테/에게/께

The case particles 한테, 에게, and 께 are one-form particles that mark the animate indirect object of the sentence, corresponding with "to" in English.

The particle 한테

The particle 한테 is most widely used in colloquial settings.

> 아버지한테 이야기해요 "(I) talk to father"
> 제 친구한테 전화 했어요 "(I) made a phone call to my friend"
> 지나한테 연락해요 "(I) contact Gina"
> 유진한테 책을 줬어요 "(I) gave books to Eugene"
> 강아지한테 우유를 줬어요 "(I) gave milk to the puppy"

Notice that the indirect objects are all animate objects (e.g., person, animals). As previously noted, the particle 에 is used if the indirect objects are inanimate objects (e.g., destinations).

> 회사에 전화해요 "(I) make a phone call to the company"
> 학교에 등록금을 내요 "(I) pay tuition to school"
> 한국에 가요 "(I) go to Korea"

The particle 에게

The particle 에게 is used instead of 한테 in more formal usage (e.g., written communication).

> 이 편지를 제임스에게 보냈습니다 "(I) sent this letter to James"

Notice that the sentence above sounds formal, since the particle 에게 as well as the deferential speech level ending 습니다 are used.

The particle 께

When the indirect object is an the esteemed person or senior, such as one's boss, teachers, and parents, the particle 께 can be optionally used instead of 한테 or 에게. The particle 께 is another indirect object particle, used to indicate honorific meanings to the esteemed indirect object. For instance, consider the following sentences:

> 선생님께 가방을 드렸어요 "(I) gave a bag to the teacher"
> 사장님께 가방을 드렸어요 "(I) gave a bag to the president"

In these examples above, the indirect objects are the teacher and the president to whom the speaker wishes to express honorific attitude. Consequently, the use of the particle 께 is more appropriate than the use of 한테 or 에게.

One thing to remember when using 께, is that since it is an honorific element its usage should be collocated with other honorific elements such as the honorific suffix, euphemistic words, proper address or reference terms and so on. For example, in the above examples, 드리다 "give (honorific)" is used instead of 주다 "give (plain form)."

The particles 한테서 and 에게서

The case particles 한테서 and 에게서 are both one-form particles. These particles mark an animate source, corresponding to "from" in English. The only difference between 한테서 and 에게서 is that the former is used in colloquial settings whereas the latter is used for a more formal context. For instance, consider the following sentences:

토니한테서 책을 받았어요 "(I) received the book from Tony"
프랭크한테서 전화를 기다려요 "(I) wait for a phone call from Frank"

존에게서 가방을 선물로 받았습니다 "(I) received the bag as a present from John"
에밀리에게서 편지를 기다립니다 "(I) wait for the letter from Emily"

Exercises

Key vocabulary for Unit 14 exercises

가르치다 to teach
도착하다 to arrive
말하다 to speak
미국 America/USA
빌리다 to borrow
어머니 mother
전화하다 to make a phone call
책 book
친구 friend
편지 letter
한국 Korea (South)

Exercise 14.1

Choose the appropriate particle from the brackets:

> Example: 학교 _____(에/에서) 공부해요 "(I) study at school."
>   = 에서

1 어디_____(에/에서) 일하세요? "Where (do you) work?"
2 오전 11시___(에/에서) 서울로 떠나요. "(I) leave for Seoul at 11 a.m."
3 공원____(에/에서) 만나요. "(Let us) meet at the park."
4 이번 주말___(에/에서) 뭐 하세요? "What (do you) do this weekend?"
5 토마스가 런던_____(에/에서) 왔어요. "Thomas came from London."
6 YMCA____(에/에서) 수영해요. "(I) swim at the YMCA."
7 제이슨은 시카고____ 일해요. "As for Jason, (he) works in Chicago."
8 학교 식당_____(에/에서) 아침을 먹어요. "(I) eat breakfast at the school cafeteria."
9 한국어 수업이 오후 3 시_____(에/에서) 있어요. "Korean class is at 3 p.m."
10 집___(에/에서) 학교까지 차로 1시간 걸려요. "(It) takes 1 hour by car from home to school."

Exercise 14.2

Fill in the blanks with the appropriate particle from the particles in the brackets:

> Example: 어머니__(한테/ 한테서) 소식을 들었어요
>   "(I) heard news from mother."
>   = 한테서

1 경찰서____(에/한테) 연락했어요. "(I) contacted the police station."
2 친구___(한테/ 한테서) 선물을 받았어요. "(I) received presents from friends."
3 할아버지___(께/ 한테/한테서) 전화 할 거예요. "(I) will make a phone call to grandfather."
4 자동응답기___(에/한테) 메세지를 남겼어요. "(I) left a message on the answering machine."
5 형 _____(한테/ 한테서) 무슨 선물을 받고 싶어요? "What kind of present (do you) want to receive from (your) older brother?"
6 어제 톰_____(한테/ 한테서) 책을 줬어요. "(I) gave books to Tom yesterday."

7 누나___(한테/ 한테서) 영어로 말하세요? "(Do you) speak in English to (your) older sister?"

8 프론트 데스크___(에/에게) 전화하십시오 "Make a phone call to the front desk."

9 대학생들___(에게/에게서) 한국어를 가르칩니다. "(I) teach Korean to college students."

10 누구 ___(에게/ 에게서) 열쇠를 받았습니까? "From whom (did you) receive the key?"

Exercise 14.3

Underline which of the two Korean translations for the English sentences below is correct in each case:

Example: "(I) gave a book to Susan"
= 수잔에 책을 줬어요/ 수잔한테 책을 줬어요

1 "(I) received the invitation from Michael."
마이클에서 초대를 받았어요 / 마이클한테서 초대를 받았어요.

2 "What time did (you) leave the hotel?"
호텔한테서 몇 시에 나갔어요? / 호텔에서 몇 시에 나갔어요?

3 "(I) heard that story from radio."
그 이야기를 라디오한테서 들었어요/ 그 이야기를 라디오에서 들었어요.

4 "(I) called Andrew yesterday."
어제 앤드류한테 전화를 했어요/ 어제 앤드류한테서 전화를 했어요.

5 "(I) sent the mail to Manager Kim last week."
지난 주에 김실장님에게서 멜을 보냈습니다 / 지난 주에 김실장님께 멜을 보냈습니다.

6 "Throw the trash into the trash basket."
쓰리기통에 쓰레기를 버리십시오/ 쓰레기통한테 쓰레기를 버리십시오.

7 "(I) borrow the book from Andrew."
앤드류한테서 책을 빌려요/ 앤드류한테 책을 빌려요.

8 "(I) hear the news from a friend."
친구한테서 소식을 들어요/ 친구에게 소식을 들어요.

9 "(I) called home."
집한테 전화했어요/ 집에 전화했어요.

10 "(I) sell cars to Koreans."
한국 사람들한테 차를 팔아요/ 한국 사람들한테서 차를 팔아요.

Exercise 14.4

Each sentence has one incorrect particle. Identify the incorrect particle
and make a correction as needed:

Example: 티모티의 형을 선생님이에요
"As for Timothy's older brother, (he) is a teacher"
= 티모티의 형은 선생님이에요

1 한국에 편지가 왔어요. "A letter arrived from Seoul."
2 학교 식당에서 친구한테 만나요. "(We) meet friend at the school cafeteria."
3 할아버지에게서 전화하세요. "Make a call to grandfather."
4 선생님이 저께 책을 주셨어요. "The teacher gave a book to me."
5 저스틴이 니콜한테서 꽃을 주었어요. "Justin gave flowers to Nicole."
6 저에 연락하세요. "Contact me."
7 학생들한테서 비디오를 보여 주세요. "(I) show the video to students."
8 부모님에 편지가 왔어요. "A letter arrived from (my) parents."

Exercise 14.5

Fill in the blanks with the appropriate particles from the following list:

은, 는, 이, 가, 의, 에, 한테, 에서, 한테서

1 제 이름_____토마스예요. "As for my name, (it) is Thomas."
2 방 안 ____ 책상____있어요. "There is a desk in the room."
3 서울____ 한국____수도예요. "Seoul is Korea's capital."
4 이 것이 캐서린____ 가방이에요. "This is Catherine's bag."
5 학교 식당____ 만나요. "(Let us) meet at the school cafeteria."
6 브라이언_____ 메세지를 전해 주세요. "Please pass the message to Brian."
7 이사벨_____편지가 도착했어요. "A letter arrived from Isabel."
8 오후 7시____ 뉴욕____가요. "(I) go to New York at 7 p.m."
9 숙제____ 도서관____해요. "As for homework, (I) do (it) at the library."
10 매일 아침 6시____조깅해요. "I jog at 6 o'clock in the morning everyday."
11 오전 8시에 집_____ 나왔어요. "I came out from home at 8 a.m."
12 오늘 사무실_____ 전화할 거예요. "(I) will make a phone call to the office today."

Exercise 14.6

Translate the following sentences into Korean.

Example: "(I) made a phone call to the office"
= 사무실에 전화했어요

1 "The letter arrived from Korea."
2 "(I) make a phone call to my mother."
3 "(I) borrowed the book from John."
4 "(I) taught Korean to American students."
5 "(Do you) speak in Korean to your friend?"

UNIT 15

Special particles 1
도 *to* and 만 *man*

In the previous units, the case particles, such as 이/가, 을/를, 에, 의, (으)로, 와/과, (이)랑, 하고, 에서, 한테, 에게, 께, 한테서, and 에게서 were discussed. The only special particle introduced so far is the topic particle 은/는. This unit discusses the difference between the case and special particles in their functions as well as the place where they appear. Then, the unit introduces two special particles, 만 and 도.

The differences between case particles and special particles

What distinguishes case particles from special particles lies in their functions. While the primary function of the case particle is to indicate the syntactic role of the noun it attaches to (e.g., whether the noun is the subject, object, indirect object, and so on), that of the special particle is to add a special meaning such as "also," "even," and "only," or to indicate whether the word it attaches to is the topic of the sentence.

Case particles also differ from special particles in the place they appear in the sentence. A case particle can appear only after a noun (e.g., subject, object, indirect objects etc.). However, a special particle can appear in one of three places. First, it can appear in place of a case particle. For instance, a special topic particle 은/는 can appear where you would expect the subject case particle 이/가:

수잔의 학생이에요 "Susan is a student"
수잔은 학생이에요 "As for Susan, (she) is a student"

오늘 날씨가 좋아요 "Today's weather is good"
오늘 날씨는 좋아요 "As for today's weather, (it) is good"

They can also appear in the place where you would expect the object case particle 을/를:

마이클이 골프를 배워요 "Michael learns golf"
마이클이 골프는 배워요 "As for golf, Michael learns (it)"

수잔이 스파게티를 좋아해요 "Susan likes spaghetti"
수잔이 스파게티는 좋아해요 "As for spaghetti, she likes (it)"

Second, a special particle can appear after an existing case particle, such as 에, 에서, and 으로, in order to add the special meaning.

브라이언이 거실에서 자요 "Brian sleeps in the living room"
브라이언이 거실에서는 자요 "As for the living room, Brian sleeps (there)"

Third, a special particle can appear not only after a noun but also after an adverb, such as 빨리 "fast" and 싸게 "cheaply; at a low price."

그 식당이 음식을 빨리 줘요 "That restaurant serves the food fast"
그 식당이 음식을 빨리는 줘요 "(I don't know about other things but) that restaurant serves the food fast"

그 가게가 과일을 싸게 팔아요 "That store sells fruit at cheap prices"
그 가게가 과일을 싸게는 팔아요 "(I don't know about other things but) that store sells fruit at a low price"

Consequently, one cannot simply memorize where a certain particle (including both case and special particles) always appears in a certain context. This is because, as seen above, a particle can appear in the place where you would expect the other particle to be.

The special particle 만

The one-form special particle 만 adds the meaning of "only" or "just" on the noun it attaches to. The special particle 만 can appear in place of the case particles 이/가 or 을/를.

나오꼬가 커피를 마셔요 "Naoko drinks coffee"
나오꼬만 커피를 마셔요 "Only Naoko drinks coffee"
나오꼬가 커피만 마셔요 "Naoko drinks only coffee"

사이몬이 한국어를 공부해요 "Simon studies Korean"
사이몬만 한국어를 공부해요 "Only Simon studies Korean"
사이몬이 한국어만 공부해요 "Simon studies only Korean"

The particle 만 can also be attached to an existing case particle, such as 에 and 에서.

앤지는 월요일에만 학교에 가요 "As for Angie, (she) goes to school only on Monday"
앤지는 월요일에 학교에만 가요 "As for Angie, (she) goes only to school on Monday"

조이스는 도서관에서 공부해요 "As for Joyce, (she) studies at the library"
조이스는 도서관에서만 공부해요 "As for Joyce, (she) studies only at the library"

The particle 만 "only" can also appear after an adverb, such as 맛있게 "deliciously" and 빨리 "fast."

맛있게 만들어 주세요 "Please cook (it) deliciously"
맛있게만 만들어 주세요 "Please just cook (it) deliciously"

빨리 오세요 "Come in hurry"
빨리만 오세요 "Just come in hurry"

The special particle 도

The one-form special particle 도 adds the meaning of "also," "too," or "even" to the noun it attaches to. Just like the particle 만, the special particle 도 can appear in place of the case particles 이/가 or 을/를.

나오꼬가 커피를 마셔요 "Naoko drinks coffee"
나오꼬도 커피를 마셔요 "Naoko also drinks coffee"
나오꼬가 커피도 마셔요 "Naoko drinks even coffee"

사이몬이 한국어를 공부해요 "Simon studies Korean"
사이몬도 한국어를 공부해요 "Even Simon studies Korean"
사이몬이 한국어도 공부해요 "Simon studies Korean as well"

The particle 도 can also be attached to an existing case particle, such as 에 and 에서.

앤지는 일요일에 일해요 "As for Angie, (she) works on Sunday"
앤지는 일요일에도 일해요 "As for Angie, (she) works even on Sunday"

조이스는 커피숍에서 공부해요 "As for Joyce, (she) studies at the coffee shop"
조이스는 커피숍에서도 공부해요 "As for Joyce, (she) studies even at the coffee shop"

The particle 도 can appear after an adverb as well.

맛있게 만들어 주세요 "Cook (it) deliciously"
맛있게도 만들어 주세요 "Cook (it) deliciously also"

Koreans use the particle 도 when they list additional items. For instance, consider the following sentences:

집에 파스타가 있어요. 그리고 와인도 있어요 "There is some pasta at home. And there are some wines too"

Notice that the speaker lists "wine" as an additional item, by using the particle 도. Here is one more example:

월요일에 요가를 해요. 그리고 수영도 해요 "On Monday, (I) do yoga. And (I) also swim"

Notice that the particle 도 also serves to add the additional activity 수영 "swimming" to the first activity 요가 "yoga."

Meanwhile, the particle 도 can also generate the emphatic meaning "even" to the noun it attaches to, as shown in the example below:

큰 집이 있어요. 그리고 빌딩도 있어요 "(They) have a big house. And (they) have even a building"

In negative sentences, the particle 도 is translated as "either." Consider the following examples:

차가 없어요. 자전거도 없어요 "(I) don't have a car. (I) don't have a bicycle either"
존은 캐나다 사람이 아니에요. 브라이언도 캐나다 사람이 아니에요 "As for John, (he) is not a Canadian. As for Brian, (he) is not a Canadian either"

Exercises

Key vocabulary for Unit 15 exercises

고기 meat
깨끗하다 to be clean
노래 song
녹차 green tea
돕다 to help

마시다 to drink
많다 to be many/a lot
맛있다 to be delicious
먹다 to eat
바지 pants
방 room
보다 to see/to watch
부르다 to call/to sing
비싸다 to be expensive

사다 to buy
손님 customer
쉬다 to rest
싸게 at a cheap price
쓰다 to use/to write
야채 vegetable
여권 passport
영화 movie
음식 food
음악 music
입다 to wear (clothes)
있다 to have/to exist

작다 to be small
조용하다 to be quiet
좋아하다 to like
주다 to give
주말 weekend
차 car
청바지 jeans
추다 to dance
축구 soccer
춤 dancing
치다 to play (instrument, sports)
팔다 to sell
피아노 piano
하다 to do
화장실 restroom

Exercise 15.1

Form each sentence using the particle 도 as shown in the example. Then, translate the sentence.

Example: 집/ 크다
          = 집도 커요 "The house is also big"

1 피아노/ 치다
2 축구/ 하다
3 에어로빅/ 하다
4 가난한 사람/ 돕다
5 노래/ 부르다
6 춤/ 추다
7 손님/ 많다
8 음식/ 맛있다
9 방/ 조용하다
10 바지/ 비싸다

Exercise 15.2

Complete each sentence using the particle 만 as shown in the example.
Then, translate the sentence.

Example: 디저트/ 맛있다
          = 디저트만 맛있어요 "Only the dessert is tasty"

1 녹차/ 마시다
2 야채/ 먹다
3 클래식 음악/ 듣다
4 코미디 영화 /보다
5 청바지/ 입다
6 주말/ 쉬다
7 방/ 깨끗하다
8 한국 음식/ 맛있다
9 화장실/ 작다
10 싸게/ 주다

Exercise 15.3

Translate the following Korean sentences into English.

Example: 브래드는 자전거도 있어요
          = "As for Brad, (he) also has a bicycle"

1 앤드류는 고기만 좋아해요.
2 애니는 일본 차도 있어요.

3 제임스는 베이스 기타도 샀어요.
4 폴은 드럼도 쳐요.
5 엘리샤만 여권이 있어요.
6 에릭만 스키를 타요.
7 캐롤라인만 노트북을 써요.
8 라처드만 학교에 갔어요.
9 로렌스만 학생이에요.
10 글렌만 레드 와인을 좋아해요.

Exercise 15.4

Complete each sentence with the appropriate particle to match the English translation provided.

> Example: 사과____(만/도) 있어요 "There are also apples"
> = 사과도 있어요

1 한국 사람____(만/도) 있어요. "There are only Korean people."
2 이 책____(만/도) 수잔 거예요? "Is this book also Susan's?"
3 시계____(만/도) 샀어요. "(I) bought only the watch."
4 소설책____(만/도) 좋아해요. "(I) like the novel too."
5 포장지____(만/도) 예뻐요. "The wrapping paper is also pretty."
6 10 분____(만/도) 더 기다리십시오. "Wait only 10 more minutes"
7 가격___(만/도) 싸요. "The price is cheap too."
8 저 사람___(만/도) 한국 사람이에요. "Only that person is a Korean."
9 콜라____(만/도) 주세요. "Give (me) only the cola."
10 존은 아침에___(만/도) 조깅을 해요. "As for John, (he) jogs only in the morning."

Exercise 15.5

Rewrite the underlined phrase using either 만 or 도 to match the English translation.

> Example: 문을 여세요 "Open the door as well"
> = 문도 여세요

1 커피를 마셔요. "(I) drink coffee as well."
2 매튜는 베이스 기타를 쳐요. "As for Matthew, (he) plays only the bass guitar."
3 도서관이 집에서 가까워요. "The library is also close from home."
4 크리스틴를 만날 거예요. "(I) will meet only Christine."

5 <u>신분증을</u> 지갑에서 꺼냈어요. "(I) took out the ID as well from the wallet."

6 <u>타이어를</u> 새 것으로 갈았어요. "(I) replaced only the tire with a new one."

7 <u>휴지를</u> 쓰레기통에 버리세요. "Throw only the wastepaper into the waste basket."

8 <u>옷 색이</u> 예뻐요. "The color of the dress is pretty too."

9 <u>가격이</u> 싸요. "The price is also cheap."

10 <u>서비스가</u> 좋았어요. "The service was good too."

UNIT 16

Special particles 2
이나 *ina*, 부터 *put'ŏ*, and 까지 *kkaji*

The particle (이)나

The special particle (이)나 is a two-form particle. 이나 appears after a noun that ends in a consonant (e.g., 점심이나), and 나 appears after a noun that ends in a vowel (e.g., 커피나). The particle indicates four different meanings depending on the context in which it is being used: (1) "or something (like that)," (2) "or," (3) "as many as," and (4) "about."

First, the particle (이)나 means "or something (like that)," when it is used after a single noun. Consider the following examples.

집에서 TV나 볼 거예요 "(I) will watch TV or something (like that)"
테니스나 쳐요 "(I) play tennis or something"
비디오 게임 이나 해요 "(Let us) play video games or something"
조깅이나 합시다 "(Let us) jog or something"
햄버거나 먹으십시오 "Eat hamburgers or something"

As seen above, the particle (이)나 marks the object of the sentence and reduces the importance of the object noun. For instance, the object being chosen may not be the best possible action or item for the given situation or there may be more choices. In addition, when the particle (이)나 is used with certain question words such as 어디 "where," 무엇 "what," and 누구 "who," the particle (이)나 reduces the interrogative meaning of these question words and generalize their meanings, as in:

어디 "where" becomes 어디나 "anywhere"
누구 "who" becomes 누구나 "whoever," "anyone," or "everyone"
무엇 "what" becomes 무엇이나 "anything" or "whatever"

어디가 맛있어요? "Where is (it) delicious?"
어디나 맛있어요 "(It) is delicious anywhere"

티파니는 누구 좋아해요? "As for Tiffany, who (does she) like?"
티파니는 누구나 좋아해요 "As for Tiffany, (she) likes anyone"

존은 뭐 먹어요? "As for John, what (does he) eat?"
존은 무엇<u>이나</u> 다 먹어요 "As for John, (he) eats about everything"

Second, when the particle (이)나 is used between two nouns, it simply means "or." Consider the following examples:

사과<u>나</u> 오렌지 주세요 "Give (me) apples or oranges"
서점<u>이나</u> 학교에 갈 거예요 "(I) will go to the bookstore or school"
커피<u>나</u> 녹차 주세요 "Give (me) coffee or green tea"

Third, when the particle (이)나 is attached to an expression of quantity, the particle means "as many as," "as much as" or "up to." The particle expresses the speaker's surprise that the quantity of the item is more than the speaker's expectation. For example, consider the following sentences:

네 시간<u>이나</u> 운전했어요 "(I) drove as many as four hours"
텔레비전을 두 시간<u>이나</u> 봐요 "(I) watch TV as many as two hours"
100 달라<u>나</u> 받았아요 "(I) received as much as 100 dollars"
이 커피가 5 불<u>이나</u> 해요 "This coffee (can) costs as much as 5 dollars"

Fourth, the particle (이)나 means "about" or "approximately," when it is used with certain question words, such as 몇 "how many" and 얼마 "how much."

이 옷은 얼마<u>나</u> 줬어요? "As for this dress, about how much did (you) give?"
차로 몇 시간<u>이나</u> 걸려요? "About how many hours does (it) take by car?"
몇 과목<u>이나</u> 들어요? "About how many classes do (you) take?"
몇 병<u>이나</u> 살 거예요? "About how many bottles will (you) buy?"
몇 사람<u>이나</u> 초대할까요? "About how many people shall (we) invite?"

Particles 부터 and 까지

The particle 부터 "from" is used to indicate a beginning temporal point. Consider the following examples:

밤 11 시<u>부터</u> 잤어요 "(I) slept from 11 o'clock at night"
밤 11 시<u>에</u> 잤어요 "(I) slept at 11 o'clock at night"

한국어 수업이 오전 10시<u>부터</u> 있어요 "There is a Korean language class from 10:00 a.m."
한국어 수업이 오전 10시<u>에</u> 있어요 "There is a Korean language class at 10:00 a.m."

We learned that the particle 에 can be used after the time expression as well. However, as seen above, while the particle 에 simply means "at," the particle 부터 "from" indicates a starting temporal point.

The particle 까지 indicates an ending point, and it corresponds to "to," "up to," "until" or "as far as" in English. When the particle is used with a place noun, it indicates an ending location (e.g., destination), as in:

뉴욕시까지 차로 세시간 걸려요 "(It) takes three hours by car to New York City"
학교까지 멀어요 "(It) is far to school"

When the particle is used with a temporal noun, it indicates an ending temporal point, as in:

오후 2시까지 기다릴 거예요 "(We) will wait until 2:00 p.m."
아침 6시까지 못 잤어요 "(I) could not sleep until 6 o'clock in the morning"

The particles 부터 and 까지 are often used together to express "from [time expression] to [time expression]."

오전 11시부터 오후 3시까지 "From 11:00 a.m. till 3:00 p.m."
아침부터 밤까지 "From morning till night"
어제부터 내일까지 "From yesterday till tomorrow"

In a similar manner, the particles 에서 and 까지 frequently show up together to indicate "from [location] to [location]."

서울에서 동경까지 "From Seoul to Tokyo"
커피숍에서 아파트까지 "From the coffee shop to the apartment"
머리에서 발톱까지 "From head to toe"

The particle 까지 can be used with a non-time and/or a non-place noun, such as persons, clothes, and so forth. When it is used with a non-place or a non-time noun, the particle 까지 means "including (even)." Consider the following examples:

바바라까지 서울에 갔어요 "Even Barbra went to Seoul"
어제 맥주까지 마셨어요 "(We) even drank beers yesterday"
벨트까지 샀어요 "(I) even bought a belt"
컴퓨터까지 팔았어요 "(I) even sold the computer"
토마스의 여자친구까지 만났어요 "(I) even met Thomas' girlfriend"

Exercises

Key vocabulary for Unit 16 exercises

가방 bag
가족 family
강 river
경찰서 police station
고장 out of order
공항 airport
교회 church
국수 noodles
기차역 train station
꽃 flower
날씨 weather
남자 man
덥다 to be hot (weather)
드라마 drama
딸 daughter
라면 ramen (a type of instant noodle)
마시다 to drink
만나다 to meet
맥주 beer
물 water

바꾸다 to change
밤 night
백화점 department store
병원 hospital
비누 soap
빨래 laundry
빵 bread
사다 to buy
산 mountain
샴푸 shampoo
설거지 dishwashing
소파 sofa
슈퍼마켓 supermarket
숟가락 spoons
신발 shoes

아들 son
아침 morning
약국 pharmacy

양복 suit
여자 woman
연필 pencil
영화 movie
오다 to come
오전 a.m.
오후 p.m.
우체국 post office
운전하다 to drive
은행 bank
음식점 restaurant
의자 chair

저녁 evening/dinner
젓가락 chopsticks
쥬스 juice
지갑 wallet
집 house
친구 friend
카드 card
커피숍 coffee shop
케이크 cake
펜 pen
포도주 wine
학교 school
할아버지 grandfather
할머니 grandmother
호텔 hotel

Exercise 16.1

Fill in the blank of each sentence with either 나 or 이나.

> Example: 집에서 텔레비전(이나/나) 볼 거예요
> "(I) will watch TV or something (like that)"
> = 집에서 텔레비전이나 볼 거예요

1 아침____(이나/나) 먹을 거예요. "(I) will eat breakfast or something."
2 조깅____(이나/나) 할 거예요. "(I) will jog or something."
3 한국어____(이나/나) 배울 거예요. "(I) will learn Korean or something."
4 햄버거 (이나/나) 먹을 거예요. "(I) will eat hamburgers or something."

5 맥주＿＿(이나/나) 마실 거예요. "(I) will drink beers or something."
6 파스타＿＿(이나/나) 시킬 거예요. "(I) will order pasta or something."
7 신문＿＿(이나/나) 읽을 거예요. "(I) will read a newspaper or something."
8 요가＿＿(이나/나) 할 거예요. "(I) will do yoga or something."
9 숙제＿＿(이나/나) 할 거예요. "(I) will do homework or something."
10 한국 영화＿＿(이나/나) 볼 거예요. "(I) will see a Korean movie or something."

Exercise 16.2

Underline which of the two Korean translations for the English sentence below is correct in each case.

Example: "Give (me) apples or oranges"
= <u>사과나 오렌지 주세요</u> / 사과하고 오렌지 주세요.

1 "(I) drove as many as two hours."
두 시간이나 운전했어요/ 두 시간만 운전했어요.
2 "About how many people (do you think) will come?"
학교에 몇 사람이나 올까요?/ 학교에 몇 사람 올까요?
3 "At home, (I) will make spaghetti or something (like that)."
집에서 스파게티나 만들래요 / 집에서 스파게티만 만들래요.
4 "(I) want to go to Canada or England."
캐나다하고 영국으로 가고 싶어요/ 캐나다나 영국으로 가고 싶어요.
5 "As for Korean food, (I) eat anything well."
한국음식은 무엇을 잘 먹어요/ 한국음식은 무엇이나 잘 먹어요.

Exercise 16.3

Fill in the blank with either 이나 or 나 and translate the phrase into English.

Example: 미국＿＿캐나다
= 미국이나 캐나다 "USA or Canada"

1 남자＿＿여자
2 뉴욕＿＿런던
3 영화＿＿드라마
4 할머니＿＿할아버지
5 딸＿＿아들

6 비누＿＿＿샴푸
7 젓가락＿＿＿숟가락
8 스파게티＿＿＿파스타
9 택시＿＿＿버스
10 소파＿＿＿의자

Exercise 16.4

Translate the following phrases into Korean.

Example: "orange or apple"
= 오렌지나 사과

1 "bag or wallet"
2 "airport or train station"
3 "flower or card"
4 "beer or wine"
5 "water or juice"
6 "department store or supermarket"
7 "bread or cake"
8 "mountain or river"
9 "pencil or pen"
10 "family or friend"

Exercise 16.5

Translate the following phrases into English.

Example: 월요일부터 수요일까지 = "From Monday till Wednesday"
서울에서 동경까지 = "From Seoul to Tokyo"

1 병원에서 학교까지
2 저녁부터 아침까지
3 공항에서 호텔까지
4 아침부터 밤까지
5 런던에서 파리까지
6 교회에서 집까지
7 은행에서 경찰서까지
8 우체국에서 커피숍까지
9 오전10시부터 오후 2시까지
10 약국에서 음식점까지

Exercise 16.6

Complete the sentence using 까지, and translate the sentence.

Example: 토마스____ 학교에 갔어요
           = 토마스까지 학교에 갔어요 "Even Thomas went to school"

 1 커피___ 마셨어요.
 2 설거지___ 했어요.
 3 에어로빅___ 했어요.
 4 보스톤___ 운전했어요.
 5 윌리엄___ 파티에 왔어요.
 6 타이어___ 새로 바꿨어요.
 7 전화___ 고장이에요.
 8 신발___ 사고 싶어요.
 9 누나___ 만났어요.
10 날씨___ 더웠어요.

UNIT 17
Past tense and double past tense marker

The past tense marker 었/았

Since the stems of verbs and adjectives cannot be used alone, they are always used with endings. Korean has many different endings that convey much of the grammatical functions such as tense, aspects, sentence types, conjunctions, speech levels, and so on. The endings can be categorized into two types: final endings and pre-final endings, depending on where they appear in the verb or adjective.

Final endings include various speech level endings, such as the polite level -어/아요 and the deferential speech level -습니다. Pre-final endings are inflectional elements that come between the stem and the final ending. Pre-final endings include the past tense marker 었/았 and the honorific suffix -(으)시. For instance, consider the following sentence:

김교수님이 한국어를 가르치셨어요 "Professor Kim taught the Korean language"

Notice the past tense marker 었 and the honorific suffix 시 appear between the stem 가르치 and the speech level ending -어요, as in 가르치셨어요 (contracted from 가르치+시었 +어요) "taught."

The past tense marker 었/았 is a two-form pre-final ending in that 았 is used after a stem that ends in a bright vowel (e.g., 아 or 오), while 었 is used after a stem that ends in all other vowels. The following list shows how the marker is placed between the stem and the polite speech level ending -어/아요.

Verb stem	Past	Polite speech level ending
가 "go"	았	어요 = 갔어요 "went" (contracted from 가았어요)
오 "come"	았	어요 = 왔어요 "came" (from 오았어요)
보 "see"	았	어요 = 봤어요 "saw" (from 보았어요)
받 "receive"	았	어요 = 받았어요 "received"
먹 "eat"	었	어요 = 먹었어요 "ate"

가르치 "teach"	었	어요 = 가르쳤어요 "taught" (from 가르치었어요)
배우다 "learn"	었	어요 = 배웠어요 "learned"
이 "copula"	었	어요 = 이었어요 (or 였어요) "was/were"
있 "exist/have"	었	어요 = 있었어요 "existed/had"
하 "do"	았	어요 = 했어요 "did" (irregular)
작 "small"	았	어요 = 작았어요 "was small"
많 "many"	았	어요 = 많았어요 "was many/much"
좁 "narrow"	았	어요 = 좁았어요 "was narrow"
크 "big"	었	어요 = 컸어요 "was big" (contracted from 크었어요)
적 "few"	었	어요 = 적었어요 "was few"

Note that -어요 is used after the past tense marker, 았/었. In addition, the conjugation of the verb 하다 "do" is irregular in that the stem 하 is changed to 해, when it is combined with the past tense marker, as in 했어요 "did."

In general, the Korean past tense is similar to the English past tense in that they both signal the past action or situation. However, there is one subtle difference between them. While the English past tense primarily indicates something that occurred in the past, the Korean past tense indicates not only something that happened in the past but also whether the action or event is complete or not. For example, consider the following sentences:

집에 왔어요 "(I) came home" or "(I) am home" (as a result of the complete action of coming home)
양말을 신었어요 "(I) wore socks" or "(I) am wearing socks" (as a result of the complete action of wearing socks)
코트를 입었어요 "(I) wore a coat" or "(I) am wearing a coat"
보름달이 떴어요 "The full moon came up" or "The full moon is up"
우리 아버지는 늙으셨어요 "As for my father, (he) is old" or "As for my father, (he) became older"

Notice that the above examples all have two interpretations. The first interpretation simply indicates something happened in the past. The second interpretation expresses the completion of an action or event. For instance, one may be at home, since the action of coming home is complete. In addition, one may be wearing socks, since the action of wearing socks is complete.

Double past tense marker 었/았었

In Korean, one can change a past sentence into a double past sentence by adding 었 to the existing past tense marker 았/었.

Verb stem	Past + Past		Polite speech level ending
가 "go"	았	었	어요 = 갔었어요 "went (and no longer here)"
오 "come"	았	었	어요 = 왔었어요 "came (and no longer here)"
보 "see"	았	었	어요 = 봤었어요 "saw (long before)"
받 "receive"	았	었	어요 = 받았었어요 "received" (long before)"
먹 "eat"	었	었	어요 = 먹었었어요 "ate (long before)"
가르치 "teach"	었	었	어요 = 가르쳤었어요 "taught (or used to teach)"
배우다 "learn"	었	었	어요 = 배웠었어요 "learned (long before)"
이 "copula"	었	었	어요 = 이었었어요 (or 였었어요) "was/were"
있 "exist/have"	었	었	어요 = 있었었어요 "existed/had (long before)"
하 "do"	았	었	어요 = 했었어요 "did (longer before)"
작 "small"	았	었	어요 = 작았었어요 "was small"
많 "many"	았	었	어요 = 많았었어요 "was many/much"
좁 "narrow"	았	었	어요 = 좁았었어요 "was narrow"
크 "big"	었	었	어요 = 컸었어요 "was big"
적 "few"	었	었	어요 = 적었었어요 "was few"

The double past tense marker 았었/었었 makes the past action or situation more remote than the regular past tense marker 았/었 does. The double past tense marker indicates that the past event is no longer relevant to the present activity or situation. In addition, it indicates that the past action or situation is totally complete. For instance, consider the following sentences.

집에 왔어요 "(I) came home" or "(I) am home"
집에 왔었어요 "(I) came home" or "(I) was home (at that time and am no longer at home)"

양말을 신었어요 "(I) wore socks" or "(I) am wearing socks"
양말을 신었었어요 "(I) wore socks" or "(I) used to wear socks"

코트를 입었어요 "(I) wore a coat" or "(I) am wearing a coat"
코트를 입었었어요 "(I) wore a coat" or "(I) used to wear a coat"

보름달이 떴어요 "The full moon came up" or "The full moon is up"
보름달이 떴었어요 "The full moon was up (back then)"

숙제 다 했어요 "(I) did all the homework" or "(I) have done all the homework"
숙제 다 했었어요 "(I) did all the homework (long before)"

데니엘은 집에 왔어요 "As for Daniel, (he) came home (and is still there)"
데니엘은 집에 왔었어요 "As for Daniel, (he) came home (and is no longer there)"

반지를 꼈어요 "(I) wore a ring" or "(I) am wearing a ring"
반지를 꼈었어요 "(I) wore a ring (no longer wear it)" or "(I) used to wear a ring"

케니가 도서관에 <u>갔어요</u> "Kenny went to the library (still gone and may come back)"

케니가 도서관에 <u>갔었어요</u> "Kenny went to the library (long time ago)"

Exercises

Key vocabulary for Unit 17 exercises

가게 store
나가다 to go out
냉장고 refrigerator
닫다 to close
도서관 library
뜨다 to float
마치다 to finish
매다 to hang/to tie
모자 hat
밤 night
배우다 to learn
버리다 to throw away
비싸다 to be expensive
빌리다 to borrow

서점 bookstore
손 hand
수박 watermelon
식탁 dining table
쓰다 to write/to use
쓰레기 garbage
씻다 to wash
아침 breakfast/morning
야구 baseball
약사 pharmacist
양복 suit
오다 to come
오후 p.m.
옷 clothes
요리 cooking
일 work
입다 to wear (clothes)

자전거 bike
좋다 to be good
좋아하다 to like

집 house
친구 friend
타다 to ride
팔다 to sell
포도주 wine
해 the sun
화장실 restroom

Exercise 17.1

Change the following sentences into past tense and translate the sentences into English.

> Example: 책하고 볼펜이 (있다)
>   = 책하고 볼펜이 있었어요 "There were a book and a pen"

1 식탁에 수박이 (있다).
2 냉장고에 오렌지가 (있다).
3 엔지가 약사 (이다).
4 줄리가 헤어 디자이너 (이다).
5 오후 5 시에 도서관에서 (나가다).
6 아침 10 시에 버스를 (타다).
7 오후 9 시에 가게를 (닫다).
8 일을 오후 6시에 (마치다).
9 친구한테서 자전거를 (빌리다).
10 화장실에서 손을 (씻다).
11 모자를 (쓰다).
12 집에 (오다).
13 해가 (뜨다).
14 넥타이를 (매다).

Exercise 17.2

Change the following sentences into double past tense and translate them.

> Example: 영화를 보다
>   = 영화를 봤었어요 "(I) saw a movie (long before)" or
>   "(I) used to see a movie"

1 유니폼을 (입다).
2 서점에서 한국어 책을 (팔다).

3 밤에 쓰레기를 (버리다).
4 이 옷은 (비싸다).
5 제니퍼의 집이 (좋다).
6 한국 노래를 (좋아하다).
7 샘이 엔지니어 (이다).
8 이 집에서 요리를 (하다).
9 야구를 (하다).
10 한국어를 (배우다).

Exercise 17.3

Change the following past or double past sentences into the present tense.

Example: 한국을 여행했어요 "(I) traveled Korea"
= 한국을 여행해요

1 친구하고 포도주를 마셨어요. "(I) drank wine with friends."
2 방이 더러웠어요. "The room was dirty."
3 날씨가 맑았어요. "The weather was clear."
4 고마웠어요. "(I) was grateful."
5 친구한테서 꽃을 받았어요. "(I) received flowers from (my) friend."
6 기차로 4 시간 걸렸었어요. "(It) used to take four hours by train."
7 인터넷으로 아버지한테 전화했었어요. "(I) used to talk to father via the internet."
8 커피숍에서 만났었어요. "(We) used to meet at the coffee shop."
9 노래를 잘 했었어요. "(I) used to sing well."
10 안경을 썼었어요. "(I) used to wear eye-glasses."

Exercise 17.4

Indicate which of the two Korean translations for the English sentence below is correct in each case:

Example: "(I) used to drive as many as two hours"
두 시간이나 운전했었어요/ 두 시간만 운전했어요

1 "As for us, (we) used to drink green teas."
우리는 녹차를 마셨어요/ 우리는 녹차를 마셨었어요.
2 "(I) listened to classical music."
클래식 음악을 들었어요/ 클래식 음악을 들었었어요.
3 "(I) am wearing a suit."
양복을 입었어요 / 양복을 입었었어요.

4 "The room was quiet."
  방이 조용했었어요/ 방이 조용했어요.
5 "The hotel used to be cheap."
  호텔이 쌌어요/ 호텔이 쌌었어요.
6 "(They) used to sell (it) inexpensively."
  싸게 팔았어요/ 싸게 팔았었어요.
7 "(He) came home (and he is home now)."
  집에 왔었어요/ 집에 왔어요.
8 "The coffee was delicious (long ago)."
  커피가 맛있어요/ 커피가 맛있었어요.
9 "(I) used to like baseball."
  야구를 좋아했었어요 / 야구를 좋아했어요.
10 "Scarlet used to be an English teacher."
  스칼릿이 영어 선생님이었어요/ 스칼릿이 영어 선생님이었었어요.

UNIT 18
Negation

Types of negative constructions

This unit discusses how to change verbs and adjectives into negatives. Korean has two ways of negating. The first is to use the negatives 안 "not" and 못 "cannot," and the use of these negatives has the short form and the long form. The second is to use the auxiliary verb 말다 "stop."

The short form negation [안/ 못 + predicate]

The negative 안 is an abbreviated form of 아니 "no," as in 아니에요 "no," or 학생이 아니에요 "(I) am not a student." In addition it is used for general negation. The negative 못 means "cannot" or "unable," and it is used for negation where one's volition or ability is involved.

One can make a short form negation by placing one of these negatives in front of the predicate, as shown below:

[안 + verb]
안 봐요   "do not see"
안 가요   "do not go"
안 먹어요   "do not eat"
안 마셔요   "do not drink"
안 배워요   "do not learn"

[안 + adjective]
안 좁아요   "is not narrow"
안 비싸요   "is not expensive"
안 작아요   "is not small"
안 커요   "is not big"
안 높아요   "is not high"

[못 + verb]
못 만들어요 "cannot make"
못 팔아요   "cannot sell"
못 자요   "cannot sleep"
못 뛰어요   "cannot run"
못 읽어요   "cannot read"

Since the negative 못 refers to one's ability or volition, it cannot be used with the adjectives which describe states or quantity. For instance, the following are ungrammatical in Korean:

비싸다   "expensive"   못 비싸요 (X)
좋다   "good"   못 좋아요 (X)
작다   "small"   못 작아요 (X)
바쁘다   "busy"   못 바빠요 (X)
즐겁다   "happy"   못 즐거워요 (X)

The short form negation is used for declarative and interrogative sentence types, but not for imperative and propositive sentence types. For instance, consider the deferential speech level that has four different endings for each sentence type:

Declarative   고기를 안 먹습니다 "(I) do not eat meat"
Interrogative 고기를 안 먹습니까? "Don't (you) eat meat?"
Imperative   고기를 안 먹으십니다 (X)
Propositive   고기를 안 먹으십시오 (X)

Declarative   커피를 못 마십니다 "(I) cannot drink coffee"
Interrogative 커피를 못 마십니까? "Can't (you) drink coffee?"
Imperative   커피를 못 마시십시다 (X)
Propositive   커피를 못 마시십시오 (X)

Meanwhile, not all verbs and adjectives can be used in the short negation form. Few verbs and adjectives that have corresponding negation verbs cannot take the short negation forms. For instance, 알다 "know" has the corresponding negation verb 모르다 "do not know." Consequently, the short form negations with 알다 such as 안 알다 or 못 알다 are grammatically wrong. Other verbs that have the corresponding negation verbs include 있다 "exist/have," 없다 "not exist/not have," and 맛있다 "delicious"/맛없다 "tasteless."

When negating compound verbs that are made of [noun + 하다], one needs to place the negative 안 or 못 in front of 하다 "do," not the whole compound verb.

요리하다	= 요리 안 해요 "(I) do not cook" (not 안 요리해요)
	= 요리 못 해요 "(I) cannot cook" (not 못 요리해요)
숙제하다	= 숙제 안 해요 "(I) do not do homework"
	= 숙제 못 해요 "(I) cannot do homework"
공부하다	= 공부 안 해요 "(I) do not study"
	= 공부 못 해요 "(I) cannot study"
운동하다	= 운동 안 해요 "(I) do not exercise"
	= 운동 못 해요 "(I) cannot exercise"
수영하다	= 수영 안 해요 "(I) do not swim"
	= 수영 못 해요 "(I) cannot swim"
조깅 하다	= 조깅 안 해요 "(I) do not jog"
	= 조깅 못 해요 "(I) cannot jog"
에어로빅하다	= 에어로빅 안 해요 "(I) do not do aerobics"
	= 에어로빅 못 해요 "(I) cannot do aerobics"
키스하다	= 키스 안 해요 "(I) do not kiss"
	= 키스 못 해요 "(I) cannot kiss"

The long form negation -지 않아요 and -지 못해요

The long form negation has the following constructions:

[stem + 지 않다]   수잔이 고기를 먹지 않아요
                    "Susan does not eat meat"
[stem + 지 못 하다] 수잔이 고기를 먹지 못 해요
                    "Susan cannot eat meat"

As seen above, the long form negation is created by adding 지 to the stem, which is followed by a negative auxiliary 않다 or 못 하다. Here are examples:

[verb stem + 지 않다]
보지 않아요   "do not see"
가지 않아요   "do not go"
먹지 않아요   "do not eat"
마시지 않아요   "do not drink"
배우지 않아요   "do not learn"

[adjective stem + 지 않다]
좁지 않아요   "is not narrow"
비싸지 않아요   "is not expensive"

작지 않아요	"is not small"
크지 않아요	"is not big"
높지 않아요	"is not high"

[verb + 지 못 하다]

만들지 못 해요	"cannot make"
팔지 못 해요	"cannot sell"
자지 못 해요	"cannot sleep"
뛰지 못 해요	"cannot run"
읽지 못 해요	"cannot read"

There is no meaning difference between the long form negation and the short form negation. Consequently they are used interchangeably. However, the long form negation tends to be more often used in written and formal communication.

Meanwhile, it was noted that the negative 못 is not used with the adjectives in the short form negation, since 못 involves one's ability or volition. However, in the long form negation 못 can be used with a few adjectives that denote one's desire, such as 충분하다 "abundant," 행복하다 "happy," 건강하다 "healthy," and 유능하다 "competent." When 못 is used with these adjectives, the negative 못 expresses a sense of disappointment rather than unability.

그 아이는 <u>튼튼하지 못 했어요</u> "(It is too bad that) For that child, (he) was not healthy"
그 부부는 <u>행복하지 못 했어요</u> "(It is too bad that) For that couple, (they) were not happy"

Notice that the negative 못 in the above sentences is not translated as "... could not" but "... was/were not." In other words, the negative 못 is used like 안 but with an emphatic meaning (or a sense of disappointment).

Just like the short form negation, the long form negation is used only for declarative and interrogative sentence types, but not for imperative and propositive sentence types.

Declarative	고기를 먹지 않습니다 "(I) do not eat meat"
Interrogative	고기를 먹지 않습니까? "Don't (you) eat meat?"
Imperative	고기를 먹지 않으십시오 (X)
Propositive	고기를 먹지 않으십니다 (X)

Declarative	커피를 마시지 못 합니다 "(I) cannot drink coffee"
Interrogative	커피를 마시지 못 합니까? "Can't (you) drink coffee?"
Imperative	커피를 마시지 못 합시다 (X)
Propositive	커피를 마시지 못 하십시오 (X)

To change the long form negation into the past, one needs to add the past tense marker 었/았 to the negative auxiliary verbs 않다 or 못 하다.

수잔이 고기를 <u>먹지 않았어요</u>	"Susan did not eat meat"
수잔이 고기를 <u>먹지 못했어요</u>	"Susan could not eat meat"

The negative auxiliary verb 말다

For imperative and propositive sentences, the negative auxiliary verb 말다 is used instead.

[stem + 지 말다]

그 영화를 <u>보지 말아요</u>	"Don't see that movie" or "(Let us) not see that movie"
그 영화를 <u>보지 마십시오</u>	"Don't see that movie"
그 영화를 <u>보지 맙시다</u>	"(Let us) not see that movie"
학교에 <u>가지 말아요</u>	"Don't go to school" or "(Let us) not go to school"
학교에 <u>가지 마십시오</u>	"Don't go to school"
학교에 <u>가지 맙시다</u>	"(Let us) not go to school"
매운 음식을 <u>먹지 말아요</u>	"Don't eat spicy food" or "(Let us) not eat spicy food"
매운 음식을 <u>먹지 마십시오</u>	"Don't eat spicy food"
매운 음식을 <u>먹지 맙시다</u>	"(Let us) not eat spicy food"
와인을 <u>마시지 말아요</u>	"Don't drink wine" or "(Let us) not drink wine"
와인을 <u>마시지 마십시오</u>	"Don't drink wine"
와인을 <u>마시지 맙시다</u>	"(Let us) not drink wine"

Notice that the stem 말 changes to 마 (as in 마십시오) and to 맙 (as in 맙시다). This is due to the fact that 말다 is a ㄹ irregular verb. In ㄹ-irregular, the stem loses ㄹ when the stem is followed by one of the following consonants: ㄴ, ㅂ, and ㅅ. The verb 말다 is a ㄹ-irregular. Consequently, the stem 말 loses ㄹ, as it is conjugated with the deferential imperative ending -십시오, and -십시다 (since the ending begins with ㅅ). The other ㄹ-irregular verbs include the verbs like 살다 "live," 알다 "know," 길다 "long," and so on.

However, with the polite speech level 어/아요, the ㄹ of the ㄹ-irrregular verb is retained. Consider the following examples:

TV 를 <u>보지 말아요</u>	"Don't watch TV"
집에 <u>가지 말아요</u>	"Don't go home"

Exercises

Key vocabulary for Unit 18 exercises

가다 to go
구두 shoes
건너다 to cross/to go over
길 road
김치 kimchi
낮잠 nap
내일 tomorrow
넣다 to insert
넥타이 necktie
노래 song
늦게 lately
담배 cigarettes
도서관 library
동전 coin

마시다 to drink
만나다 to meet
말하다 to speak
매다 to wear (a tie)
먹다 to eat
문 door
물 water
바쁘다 to be busy
방 room
버리다 to throw away
병원 hospital
보내다 to send
부르다 to call out/to sing
비싸다 to be expensive
비행기 airplane
빌리다 to borrow

사다 to buy
술 liquor
쉬다 to rest
식당 cafeteria
신다 to wear (shoes)
쓰다 to use/to write
쓰레기 garbage
씻다 to wash
아버지 father

안경 eye-glasses
약 medicine
얼굴 face
열다 to open
야채 vegetables
오늘 today
요가 yoga
운동 sport/exercise
운전 driving
음식 food
일어나다 to get up

저녁 dinner/evening
전화하다 to make a phone call
주말 weekend
짜다 to be salty
청소하다 to clean up
춥다 to be cold
크게 aloud
크다 to be big
타다 to ride
편지 letter
팔다 to sell
피우다 to smoke

Exercise 18.1

Change the following verb or adjective into the short form negation using the negative 안. Then translate the sentence.

Example: 텔레비전을 (보다)
= 텔레비전을 안 봐요 "(I) do not watch TV"

1 김치를 (사다)
2 저녁을 (먹다)
3 물을 (마시다)
4 방을 (청소하다)
5 구두를 (신다)
6 주말에 (바쁘다)
7 오늘은 (춥다)
8 방이 (크다)
9 음식이 (짜다)
10 야채가 (비싸다)

Exercise 18.2

Change the following verb or adjective into the short form negation using the negative 못. Then translate the sentence.

> Example: 공포 영화를 (보다)
> = 공포 영화를 못 봐요 "(I) cannot see a horror movie"

1 내일 파티에 (가다)
2 도서관에서 책을 (빌리다)
3 김치를 (먹다)
4 아버지한테 (전화하다)
5 안경을 (쓰다)
6 넥타이를 (매다)
7 비행기를 (타다)
8 운동을 (하다)
9 주말에 (쉬다)
10 문을 (열다)

Exercise 18.3

Answer the following questions with the long form negation.

> Example: 햄버거 먹어요? "(Do you) eat hamburgers?"
> = 아니오, 먹지 않아요 "No, (I) do not eat (it)"

1 한국어를 배워요? "(Do you) learn Korean?"
2 시험이 어려워요? "Is the test difficult?"
3 주말에 일해요? "(Do you) work over the weekend?"
4 날씨가 따뜻해요? "Is the weather warm?"
5 배가 고파요? "(Are you) hungry (lit., is the stomach empty)?"
6 피곤해요? "(Are you) tired?"
7 재즈를 좋아해요? "(Do you) like jazz?"
8 커피를 마셨어요? "(Did you) drink coffee?"
9 우체국에서 만났어요? "(Did you) meet (him/her) at the post office?"
10 주말에 영화를 봤어요? "(Did you) see the movie over the weekend?"

Exercise 18.4

Make these sentences negative (imperative) using the deferential speech level ending and translate the sentence.

  Example: 학교에 (가다)
       = 학교에 가지 마십시오 "Don't go to school"

 1 쓰레기를 (버리다)
 2 담배를 (피우다)
 3 술을 (마시다)
 4 길을 (건너다)
 5 운전을 (하다)
 6 낮잠을 (자다)
 7 노래를 (부르다)
 8 얼굴을 (씻다)
 9 약을 (먹다)
10 크게 (말하다)

Exercise 18.5

Make these sentences negative (propositive) using the deferential speech level ending and translate the sentence.

  Example: 학교에 (가다)
       = 학교에 가지 맙시다 "(Let us) not go to school"

 1 늦게 (일어나다)
 2 내일 (만나다)
 3 커피를 (마시다)
 4 편지를 (보내다)
 5 차를 (팔다)
 6 옷을 (사다)
 7 동전을 (넣다)
 8 병원에 (가다)
 9 요가를 (하다)
10 학교 식당 음식을 (먹다)

Exercise 18.6

Underline the correct translation of the sentence.

Example: "(I) don't eat breakfast"
= <u>아침을 안 먹어요</u>/ 아침을 먹지 맙시다 / 아침을 먹지 말아요

1 "(I) do not know the name."
   이름을 안 알아요/ 이름을 몰라요 / 이름을 알지 않아요.
2 "The coffee is tasteless."
   커피가 안 맛있어요/ 커피가 맛없어요/ 커피가 맛있지 않아요.
3 "There is no book."
   책이 없어요/ 책이 있지 않아요/ 책이 안 있어요.
4 "(We) did not meet the father."
   아버지를 만나지 못 했어요/ 아버지를 만나지 않아요/ 아버지를 안 만
   났어요.
5 "The weather is not cold."
   날씨가 못 추워요/ 날씨가 춥지 말아요/ 날씨가 안 추워요.
6 "(Let us) not sell the car."
   차를 팔지 맙시다 / 차를 팔지 마십시오/ 차를 안 팔아요.

Exercise 18.7

One of three Korean translations is wrong. Underline the incorrect translation.

Example: "(I) can not drink coffee"
         커피를 못 마셔요/ 커피를 마시지 못 해요/ <u>커피를 못 마십시오</u>.

1 "(I) do not study."
   안 공부해요/ 공부 안 해요/ 공부하지 않아요.
2 "The weather is not cold."
   날씨가 춥지 않아요/ 날씨가 안 추워요/ 날씨가 못 추워요.
3 "Do not see the movie."
   영화를 보지 마십시오/ 영화를 보지 말아요/ 영화를 보지 않아요.
4 "(We) did not swim yesterday."
   어제 수영 안 했어요/ 어제 수영 못 했어요/ 어제 수영 하지 않았어요.
5 "The room is not clean."
   방이 깨끗하지 않아요/ 방이 안 깨끗해요 / 방이 깨끗해요.
6 "Don't (you) go home?"
   집에 안 가요? / 집에 가지 않아요? / 집에 갔어요?

UNIT 19
Irregular verbs

Korean predicates (e.g., verbs and adjectives) are either regular or irregular. The regularity of a predicate depends on whether the stem of the predicate is subject to variation. The predicates whose stem do not change, regardless of the sound of the following suffix, are called regular predicates. On the other hand, those predicates whose stems are subject to variation depending on the sound of the following suffix are called irregular predicates. This unit introduces seven irregular predicates: ㄷ-irregular, ㅂ-irregular, ㄹ-irregular, ㅇ-irregular, 르-irregular, ㅎ-irregular, and ㅅ-irregular.

ㄷ-irregular

Some verbs whose stem end with ㄷ are irregular. For instance, consider the verb 묻다. ㄷ of the stem 묻 changes to ㄹ when followed by a suffix that begins with a vowel, as shown below:

	-습니다	-어/아요
묻다 "ask"	묻습니다	물어요

Here are more examples of ㄷ-irregulars:

		-습니다	-어/아요
걷다	"walk"	걷습니다	걸어요
깨닫다	"realize"	깨닫습니다	깨달아요
듣다	"listen"	듣습니다	들어요
싣다	"load"	싣습니다	실어요

Meanwhile, not all verbs that end with ㄷ are irregular. The following are examples of regular predicates:

	-습니다	-어/아요
닫다 "close"	닫습니다	닫아요
받다 "receive"	받습니다	받아요
믿다 "believe"	믿습니다	믿어요
얻다 "gain"	얻습니다	얻어요

Notice that these ㄷ-ending verbs conjugate regularly. The stems of these regular predicates do not undergo any change whether the ensuing suffix begins with a vowel or a consonant.

ㅂ-irregular

The ㅂ-irregular predicates are subject to the following variation: ㅂ changes to either 우 or 오 (for a few predicates), when the ensuing suffix begins with a vowel. For instance, consider how 춥다 "cold" is conjugated: 춥 + 어요 = 추우 + 어요 = 추워요. Here are more examples:

	-습니다	-어/아요
굽다 "roast"	굽습니다	구워요 (구우 + 어요)
눕다 "lie down"	눕습니다	누워요 (누우 + 어요)
돕다 "help"	돕습니다	도와요 (도오 + 아요)
줍다 "pick up"	줍습니다	주워요 (주우 + 어요)
가볍다 "light"	가볍습니다	가벼워요 (가벼우 + 어요)
고맙다 "thankful"	고맙습니다	고마워요 (고마우 + 어요)
곱다 "pretty"	곱습니다	고와요 (고오 + 아요)
그립다 "longed-for"	그립습니다	그리워요 (그리우 + 어요)
더럽다 "dirty"	더럽습니다	더러워요 (더러우 + 어요)
덥다 "hot"	덥습니다	더워요 (더우 + 어요)
두렵다 "scary"	두렵습니다	두려워요 (두려우 + 어요)
뜨겁다 "heated"	뜨겁습니다	뜨거워요 (뜨거우 + 어요)
맵다 "spicy"	맵습니다	매워요 (매우 + 어요)
무겁다 "heavy"	무겁습니다	무거워요 (무거우 + 어요)
무섭다 "fearful"	무섭습니다	무서워요 (무서우 + 어요)
밉다 "hateful"	밉습니다	미워요 (미우 + 어요)
사랑스럽다 "lovely"	사랑스럽습니다	사랑스러워요 (사랑스러우 + 어요)
쉽다 "easy"	쉽습니다	쉬워요 (쉬우 + 어요)
싱겁다 "tasteless"	싱겁습니다	싱거워요 (싱거우 + 어요)
어둡다 "dark"	어둡습니다	어두워요 (어두우 + 어요)
어렵다 "difficult"	어렵습니다	어려워요 (어려우 + 어요)
아름답다 "beautiful"	아름답습니다	아름다워요 (아름다우 + 어요)
어지럽다 "dizzy"	어지럽습니다	어지러워요 (어지러우 + 어요)
즐겁다 "delightful"	즐겁습니다	즐거워요 (즐거우 + 어요)

차갑다 "cold"   차갑습니다   차가워요 (차가우 + 어요)
춥다 "cold"   춥습니다   추워요 (추우 + 어요)

Not all predicates that end with ㅂ are irregular. The followings are regular ㅂ-ending predicates:

	-습니다	-어/아요
뽑다 "extract"	뽑습니다	뽑아요
씹다 "chew"	씹습니다	씹어요
업다 "carry (on the back)"	업습니다	업어요
입다 "wear"	입습니다	입어요
잡다 "catch"	잡습니다	잡아요
접다 "fold"	접습니다	접어요
좁다 "narrow"	좁습니다	좁아요
집다 "pick up"	집습니다	집어요

ㅅ-irregular

Some verbs that end with ㅅ are subject to the following irregular conjugation: ㅅ of the stem gets deleted when followed by a suffix that begins with a vowel. Examples of ㅅ-irregular verbs are as follows:

	-습니다	-어/아요
긋다 "draw"	긋습니다	그어요
낫다 "get better"	낫습니다	나아요
붓다 "swell"	붓습니다	부어요
잇다 "connect"	잇습니다	이어요
젓다 "stir"	젓습니다	저어요
짓다 "build"	짓습니다	지어요

Not all predicates that end with ㅅ are irregular. The following are regular ㅅ-ending predicates:

	-습니다	-어/아요
벗다 "take off"	벗습니다	벗어요
빗다 "comb"	빗습니다	빗어요
빼앗다 "take (by force)"	빼앗습니다	빼앗아요
씻다 "wash"	씻습니다	씻어요
웃다 "laugh"	웃습니다	웃어요

ㅎ-irregular

Some predicates that end with ㅎ are subject to the following irregular conjugation: ㅎ of the stem drops out when followed by a suffix that begins with a vowel. A number of color-related adjectives as well as demonstratives fall into this group of irregular predicates, as shown below:

	-습니다	-어/아요
까맣다 "black"	까맣습니다	까매요
노랗다 "yellow"	노랗습니다	노래요
빨갛다 "red"	빨갛습니다	빨개요
파랗다 "blue"	파랗습니다	파래요
하얗다 "white"	하얗습니다	하얘요
그렇다 "be that way"	그렇습니다	그래요
어떻다 "be how"	어떻습니다	어때요
이렇다 "be this way"	이렇습니다	이래요
저렇다 "be that way"	저렇습니다	저래요

Regular ㅎ-ending predicates include the following:

넣다 "insert"	넣습니다	넣어요
놓다 "place"	놓습니다	놓아요
좋다 "good"	좋습니다	좋아요

르-irregular

Most Korean predicates that end with 르 conjugate irregularly: 르 of the stem drops out and a consonant ㄹ is added, when followed by a suffix that begins either 어 or 아. For instance, consider the verb 가르다 "divide." Notice that 르 of the stem is deleted but a consonant ㄹ is inserted, when followed by polite speech level ending -아요:

	-ㅂ니다	-어/아요
가르다	가릅니다	갈라요 (가르 + 아요 = 갈 ㄹ + 아요 = 갈라요)

Here are more examples:

	-ㅂ니다	-어/아요
고르다 "choose"	고릅니다	골라요
구르다 "roll (over)"	구릅니다	굴러요
기르다 "foster"	기릅니다	길러요
나르다 "carry"	나릅니다	날라요

누르다 "press"	누릅니다	눌러요
두르다 "put around"	두릅니다	둘러요
마르다 "dry (up)"	마릅니다	말라요
모르다 "do not know"	모릅니다	몰라요
바르다 "paste"	바릅니다	발라요
부르다 "sing/call out"	부릅니다	불러요
앞지르다 "get ahead of"	앞지릅니다	앞질러요
어지르다 "disarrange"	어지릅니다	어질러요
엎지르다 "spill"	엎지릅니다	엎질러요
오르다 "go up"	오릅니다	올라요
자르다 "cut (off)"	자릅니다	잘라요
찌르다 "pierce"	찌릅니다	찔러요
흐르다 "flow"	흐릅니다	흘러요
게으르다 "lazy"	게으릅니다	게을러요
다르다 "different"	다릅니다	달라요
배부르다 "full"	배부릅니다	배불러요
빠르다 "fast"	빠릅니다	빨라요
서투르다 "unskillful"	서투릅니다	서툴러요

It must be noted that the irregular conjugation of 르-irregular happens only after two vowels, 어 and 아, but not with other vowels.

	-ㅂ니다	-어/아요	-으니까	-ㄹ래요
가르다 "divide"	가릅니다	갈라요	가르니까	가를래요

Not all predicates that end with 르 are subject to this irregular conjugation. The following few 르-ending predicates are regular:

	-ㅂ니다	-어/아요
다다르다 "arrive at"	다다릅니다	다다라요
따르다 "follow"	따릅니다	따라요
치르다 "pay off"	치릅니다	치러요

ㄹ-irregular

All Korean predicates that end in ㄹ are subject to the following irregular conjugation: ㄹ drops out when the following suffix begins with one of ㄴ, ㅂ, and ㅅ.

	-ㅂ니다	-어/아요	-는	-세요
갈다 "grind"	갑니다	갈아요	가는	가세요
걸다 "hang"	겁니다	걸어요	거는	거세요

날다 "fly"	납니다	날아요	나는	나세요
놀다 "play"	놉니다	놀아요	노는	노세요
달다 "hang (up)"	답니다	달아요	다는	다세요
돌다 "turn (around)"	돕니다	돌아요	도는	도세요
떠들다 "make a noise"	떠듭니다	떠들어요	떠드는	떠드세요
떨다 "tremble"	떱니다	떨어요	떠는	떠세요
만들다 "make"	만듭니다	만들어요	만드는	만드세요
말다 "roll up"	맙니다	말아요	마는	마세요
물다 "bite (at)"	뭅니다	물어요	무는	무세요
밀다 "push"	밉니다	밀어요	미는	미세요
벌다 "earn"	법니다	벌어요	버는	버세요
불다 "blow (up)"	붑니다	불어요	부는	부세요
빌다 "beg"	빕니다	빌어요	비는	비세요
살다 "live"	삽니다	살아요	사는	사세요
쓸다 "sweep"	씁니다	쓸어요	쓰는	쓰세요
알다 "know"	압니다	알아요	아는	아세요
얼다 "freeze"	업니다	얼어요	어는	어세요
열다 "open"	엽니다	열어요	여는	여세요
울다 "cry"	웁니다	울어요	우는	우세요
털다 "shake off"	텁니다	털어요	터는	터세요
팔다 "sell"	팝니다	팔아요	파는	파세요
풀다 "untie"	풉니다	풀어요	푸는	푸세요
헐다 "destroy"	헙니다	헐어요	허는	허세요
흔들다 "shake"	흔듭니다	흔들어요	흔드는	흔드세요
길다 "long"	깁니다	길어요	긴	기세요
가늘다 "thin"	가늡니다	가늘어요	가는	가느세요
달다 "sweet"	답니다	달아요	단	–
멀다 "far"	멉니다	멀어요	먼	–
질다 "watery"	집니다	질어요	진	–

으 irregular

All Korean predicates that ends with the vowel 으 are subject to the following irregular conjugation: the vowel 으 of the stem drops out when the following suffix begins with a vowel.

	-ㅂ니다	-어/아요
끄다 "put off"	끕니다	꺼요 (ㄲ + 어요)
담그다 "soak (in)"	담급니다	담가요 (담ㄱ + 아요)
따르다 "follow"	따릅니다	따라요 (따 ㄹ + 아요)
뜨다 "float"	뜹니다	떠요 (ㄸ + 어요)
쓰다 "write, use"	씁니다	써요 (ㅆ + 어요)

고프다 "hungry"	고픕니다	고파요 (고 ㅍ + 아요)
기쁘다 "happy"	기쁩니다	기뻐요 (기 ㅃ + 어요)
나쁘다 "bad"	나쁩니다	나빠요 (나 ㅃ + 아요)
바쁘다 "busy"	바쁩니다	바빠요 (바 ㅃ + 아요)
슬프다 "sad"	슬픕니다	슬퍼요 (슬 ㅍ + 어요)
아프다 "sick"	아픕니다	아파요 (아 ㅍ + 아요)
예쁘다 "pretty"	예쁩니다	예뻐요 (예 ㅃ + 어요)
크다 "big"	큽니다	커요 (ㅋ + 어요)

Exercises

Key vocabulary for Unit 19 exercises

가방 bag
강아지 puppy
건물 building
고기 meat
공 ball
공책 notebook
기분 feeling/mood
길 road
껌 gum
꽃병 flower vase

노래 song
돈 money
모자 hat/cap
목 throat
물 water
바람 wind
배 stomach/ship
산 mountain
색 color
선생님 teacher

어머니 mother
얼굴 face
이야기 story
자동차 car
줄 line
짐 load/burden
책 book
친구 friend
하늘 sky

Exercise 19.1

Change the dictionary form into the deferential speech level. Then translate the sentence.

> Example: 학교에 (가다)
>   = 학교에 갑니다 "(I) go to school"

1 선생님한테 (묻다)
2 고기를 (굽다)
3 책이 (무겁다)
4 꽃병에 물을 (붓다)
5 하늘이 (파랗다)
6 강아지를 (기르다)
7 스파게티를 (만들다)
8 서울에서 (살다)
9 공이 물에 (뜨다)
10 배가 (고프다)

Exercise 19.2

Change the dictionary form into the polite speech level. Then translate the sentence.

> Example: 학교에 (가다)
>   = 학교에 가요 "(I) go to school"

1 친구하고 길을 (걷다)
2 어머니한테서 돈을 (받다)
3 가방이 (가볍다)
4 껌을 (씹다)
5 건물을 (짓다)
6 코트를 (벗다)
7 얼굴이 (까맣다)
8 짐을 (나르다)
9 커피를 (팔다)
10 수잔이 (바쁘다)

Exercise 19.3

Write the dictionary form of the following irregular verbs.

> Example: 날씨가 더워요 "The weather is hot"
> = 덥다

1 한국 노래를 들어요. "(I) listen to Korean songs."
2 형의 이야기를 믿어요. "(I) believe (my) older brother's story."
3 커피가 차가워요. "The coffee is cold."
4 산이 아름다워요. "The mountain is beautiful."
5 공책에 줄을 그어요. "(I) draw a line on the notebook."
6 자동차 색이 하얘요. "The car's color is white."
7 얼굴에 로션을 발라요. "(I) apply the lotion to my face."
8 바람이 붑니다. "The wind blows."
9 디자인이 예뻐요. "The design is pretty."
10 목이 아파요. "The throat is sour."

Exercise 19.4

Each Korean sentence has an incorrect verb conjugation. Make a correction as needed.

> Example: 시험이 어렵어요 "The test is hard"
> = 시험이 어려워요

1 트렁크에 가방을 싣어요. "(I) load the bag into the trunk."
2 머리가 어지럽어요. "The head is dizzy."
3 김치가 맵워요. "Kimchi is spicy."
4 방이 어둡어요. "The room is dark."
5 병이 낫아요. "The illness is healed."
6 모자 색이 노랗요. "The hat's color is yellow."
7 노래를 부러요. "(I) sing a song."
8 공항이 집에서 멀습니다. "The airport is far from the home."
9 코트는 벽에 걸습니다. "As for the coat, (I) hang it on the wall."
10 요즘 바쁘아요. "(I) am busy nowadays."

UNIT 20

Expressing desire -고 싶다 *-ko sip'ta* and progressive form -고 있다 *-ko itta*

Expressing desire -고 싶다

In English, verbs such as "want" and "wish" are used to express one's desire, as in "I want to sleep" or "I wish to buy it." In Korean, -고 싶다, consisting of a connector -고 and the auxiliary adjective 싶다, is used to express the first person's desire or wish.

한국어를 <u>배우고 싶어요</u> "(I) want to learn Korean"
액션 영화를 <u>보고 싶어요</u> "(I) want to see an action movie"
한국 음식을 <u>먹고 싶어요</u> "(I) want to eat Korean food"
디지탈 카메라를 <u>사고 싶어요</u> "(I) want to buy a digital camera"
선생님을 <u>만나고 싶어요</u> "(I) wish to meet the professor"

Since one cannot speak for the second person's desire, -고 싶다 cannot be used for a second person statement. However it can be used for second person questions.

무슨 영화를 <u>보고 싶어요</u>? "What kind of movie do (you) want to see?"
어디에 <u>가고 싶어요</u>? "Where do (you) like to go?"
무슨 운동을 <u>하고 싶어요</u>? "What kind of sport do (you) like to play?"
어떤 색의 안경을 <u>쓰고 싶어요</u>? "What color of glasses do (you) like to wear?"
이번 주말에 뭐 <u>먹고 싶어요</u>? "What do (you) want to eat this weekend?"

To indicate the third person's wish in both statements and questions, -고 싶어하다 is used:

수지가 한국에 <u>가고 싶어해요</u> "Suzie wants to go to Korea"
앤드류가 스파게티를 <u>먹고 싶어해요</u> "Andrew wants to eat spaghetti"

제니퍼가 집에 <u>가고 싶어해요</u>? "Does Jennifer want to go home?"
존이 한국 영화를 <u>보고 싶어해요?</u> "Does John want to see a Korean movie?"

To express past tense, the past tense marker is added to the stem of the auxiliary adjective 싶다.

책을 <u>읽고 싶었어요</u> "(I) wanted to read a book"
한국에 <u>가고 싶었어요</u> "(I) wanted to go to Korea"
집에서 <u>쉬고 싶었어요</u> "(I) wanted to rest at home"
매튜가 스키를 <u>타고 싶어했어요</u> "Matthew wanted to ski"
캐티가 중국 음식을 <u>먹고 싶어했어요</u> "Cathy wanted to eat Chinese food"

Notice that the sentences above all have the past tense marker 었 attached to the stem of 싶다 (as in 싶 + 었 + 어요 = 싶었어요) or 싶어하다 (as in 싶어하 + 었 + 어요 = 싶어했어요).

To express the honorific meaning, the honorific suffix -(으)시 is added to the stem of 싶다 (as in 싶 + 으시 + 어요 = 싶으세요).

무엇을 <u>마시고 싶으세요</u>? "What would (you) like to drink?"
어디에 <u>가고 싶으세요</u>? "Where would (you) like to go?"
어느 차를 <u>사고 싶으세요</u>? "Which car would (you) like to buy?"
무슨 영화를 <u>보고 싶으세요</u>? "What kind of movie would (you) like to see?"

One thing to remember is that -고 싶다 and -고 싶어하다 do not take the copula 이다 "be." For saying "(I) want to be a teacher," the verb 되다 "become" is used instead, as in 선생님이 되고 싶어요. A sentence like 선생님이 이고 싶어요 is ungrammatical. This contrasts with English since sentences like "I want to be a teacher" and "I want to become a teacher" are both possible.

저는 엔지니어가 <u>되고 싶어요</u> "As for me, (I) want to become an engineer"
저는 변호사가 <u>되고 싶었어요</u> "As for me, (I) wanted to become a lawyer"
수잔은 선생님이 <u>되고 싶어해요</u> "As for Susan, (she) wants to become a teacher"
피터는 의사가 <u>되고 싶어했어요</u> "As for Peter, (he) wanted to become a doctor"

Progressive form -고 있다

The progressive form is used to express an action in progress. The English progressive form takes a copula ("am," "is," and "are") and a verb with "-ing," as in "John is sleeping." The Korean progressive form takes -고 있다. For instance, consider the following sentences:

피터가 한국어를 배우고 있어요 "Peter is learning Korean"
매릴린이 피자를 먹고 있어요 "Marilyn is eating a pizza"
토마스가 영화를 보고 있어요 "Thomas is seeing a movie"
수잔이 YMCA에서 운동하고 있어요 "Susan is exercising at the YMCA"

To express a past action that was in progress, the past tense marker 었/았 is added to the stem of 있다 as in, 책을 읽고 있었어요 "(I) was reading a book." Here are more examples.

테렌스가 영어를 가르치고 있었어요 "Terrence was teaching English"
제시카가 노래를 부르고 있었어요 "Jessica was singing a song"
찰스가 라디오를 듣고 있었어요 "Charles was listening to the radio"
이사벨이 거실에서 자고 있었어요 "Susan was sleeping in the living room"

To express respect to the subject, the verb 계시다 (-고 계세요) is used instead of 있다 (-고 있어요).

교수님이 전화를 하고 계세요 "The professor is making a phone call"
사장님이 손님을 만나고 계세요 "The president is meeting the guest"
어머니가 케이크를 만들고 계세요 "Mother is making a cake"
과장님이 손을 씻고 계세요 "The section chief is washing his hands"

To negate a progressive form, one can use either a short form negation or a long form negation. For example, 가게 문을 열고 있어요 "(They) are opening the store door" can be negated both in the short and long form:

short form negation [안/ 못 + predicate]
가게 문을 안 열고 있어요 "(They) are not opening the store door"

long form negation [stem + 지 않다/지 못 하다]
가게 문을 열고 있지 않아요 "(They) are not opening the store door"

Exercises

Key vocabulary for Unit 20 exercises

가다 to go
가르치다 to teach
기다리다 to wait
교수님 professor
끝내다 to finish
끓이다 to boil
나가다 to go out
노래 song
놀다 to play
다니다 to attend
대학교 university/college
돈 money
돕다 to help
되다 to become
듣다 to listen

마시다 to drink
만나다 to meet
만들다 to make
말하다 to speak/to talk
모으다 to collect/to save
물 water
믿다 to believe
바지 pants
밖 outside
받다 to receive
배우다 to learn
벗다 to take off
벌다 to earn
병원 hospital
부르다 to sing/to call out
부엌 kitchen
부치다 to mail out
빌리다 to borrow

사귀다 to make (friends)
사다 to buy
사람 person/people
살다 to live
손 hand

쉬다 to rest
시키다 to order
씻다 to wash
아버지 father
얼굴 face
영어 English
우체국 post office
운동 sport/exercise
운전하다 to drive
음식 food
의견 opinion
의사 medical doctor
일 work
입다 to wear (clothes)

자다 to sleep
자동차 car
집 house
책 book
친구 friend
타다 to ride
편지 letter
하다 to do
한국 Korea
할머니 grandmother

Exercise 20.1

Change each sentence with -고 싶다, and translate the sentence.

> Example: 학교에 (가다)
> = 학교에 가고 싶어요 "(I) want to go to school"

1 일을 (끝내다)
2 밖에 (나가다)
3 영어를 (가르치다)
4 돈을 (벌다)
5 병원에 (가다)
6 "A" 를 (받다)
7 친구를 (사귀다)
8 집에서 (쉬다)
9 운동을 (하다)
10 버스를 (타다)

Exercise 20.2

Using the words supplied below construct a sentence (e.g., the third person's desire). Then translate the sentence as shown in the example:

   Example: 토마스, 사과, 먹다
                 = 토마스가 사과를 먹고 싶어해요 "Thomas wants to eat
                 an apple"

 1 마리아, 대학교, 다니다
 2 스티븐, 의사, 되다
 3 알렉스, 할머니, 만나다
 4 리사, 오렌지 주스, 마시다
 5 로라, 코트, 벗다
 6 데이빗, 자동차, 사다
 7 니콜라스, 돈, 모으다
 8 레이첼, 친구, 돕다
 9 조셉, 친구 말, 믿다
10 루이스, 한국어, 배우다

Exercise 20.3

Translate the following sentences into Korean, using -고 싶다 or -고 싶어하다.

   Example: "(I) want to eat pizza"
                 = 피자를 먹고 싶어요

 1 "(I) want to wash my hands."
 2 "(I) want to listen to the Korean song."
 3 "(I) want to live in Seoul."
 4 "(I) wanted to receive 'A.'"
 5 "(I) wanted to speak in Korean."
 6 "(He) wants to ride a taxi."
 7 "(He) wanted to borrow a book."
 8 "(She) wants to rest."
 9 "(She) wanted to order the steak."
10 "(They) want to sing Korean songs."

Exercise 20.4

Change the verb into the progressive form and translate the sentence.

Example: 학교에서 공부해요
= 학교에서 공부하고 있어요 "(I) am studying at school"

1 매튜는 집에서 자요.
2 우체국에서 편지를 부쳐요.
3 친구 자동차를 운전해요.
4 부엌에서 음식을 만들어요.
5 물을 끓여요.
6 아버지를 기다려요.
7 사람들의 의견을 모아요.
8 밖에서 놀아요.
9 얼굴을 씻어요.
10 바지를 입어요.

Exercise 20.5

Underline which of the Korean translations matches the English sentence.

Example: "Mother is making cookies."
어머니가 쿠키를 만들어요/ <u>어머니가 쿠키를 만들고 계세요</u>

1 "Erica is meeting John at the library."
에리카가 존을 도서관에서 만나고 있어요 / 에리카가 존을 도서관
에서 만나고 있었어요.
2 "Brian is making a phone call to the professor."
브라이언이 교수님한테 전화를 해요/ 브라이언이 교수님한테 전화
를 하고 있어요.
3 "Megan is selecting a dress at the department store."
메건이 백화점에서 옷을 고르고 있어요/ 메건이 백화점에서 옷을 고
르고 있었어요.
4 "Aaron is seeing a movie with Kimberly."
아론이 킴벌리하고 영화를 봐요/ 아론이 킴벌리하고 영화를 보고 있
어요.
5 "(I) am eating pizza at Daniel's home."
데니엘 집에서 피자를 먹고 계세요/ 데니엘 집에서 피자를 먹고
있어요.
6 "(I) was drinking coffee with (my) older brother."
형하고 커피를 마시고 있어요/ 형하고 커피를 마시고 있었어요.

7 "Our team is winning."
   우리 팀이 이기고 있어요/ 우리 팀이 이기고 있었어요.
8 "(We) were singing at Karaoke."
   가라오케에서 노래를 부르고 있어요/ 가라오케에서 노래를 부르고
   있었어요.
9 "Grandfather is jogging."
   할아버지가 조깅을 하고 계세요/ 할아버지가 조깅을 하고 있어요.
10 "Father is working at the company."
   아버지가 회사에서 일해요/ 아버지가 회사에서 일하고 계세요.

UNIT 21

The endings -(으)ㄹ 거예요 *-(ŭ)l kŏyeyo* and -(으)ㄹ까요? *-(ŭ)l kkayo?*

Probable future -(으)ㄹ 거예요

In English, future tense is marked by "will" or the "be going to" pattern, as in "I will go to Chicago," or "I am going to eat pizza tonight." In Korean, the most common way to express a future event is to use the probable future ending -(으)ㄹ 거예요. One must remember however that this ending does not express *future* but *probable future*. In Korean, an event that will surely happen in the future is expressed by the present tense with a time adverb. Consider the following three sentences:

한국에 가요 "(I) go to Korea"
내일 한국에 가요 "(I) go to Korea tomorrow"
내일 한국에 <u>갈 거예요</u> "(I) will (probably) go to Korea tomorrow"

Notice that the first and the second sentences have the present tense. However, the second sentence differs from the first sentence in that it expresses the future event with the time adverb 내일 "tomorrow." The third sentence uses the probable future ending -(으) ㄹ 거예요. Notice that the possibility that the future event (e.g., going to Korea) will occur in the future is less certain in the third sentence, when compared to the second sentence. In other words, -(으)ㄹ 거예요 indicates "a probable future event" rather than "a definite future event."

The -(으)ㄹ 거예요 ending consists of three elements: -(으)ㄹ + 거 + 예요. The prospective modifier "-(으)ㄹ" indicates "future" or "uncertainty." The bound noun 거 is a colloquial form of 것 "thing" or "fact." The ending 예요 is the polite speech level ending of the copular 이다.

-(으)ㄹ 거예요 is a three-form ending: -을 거예요 is used for the verb and/or adjective stem that ends in a consonant (as in 먹을 거예요 "will eat"), and -ㄹ 거예요 is used for the verb and/or adjective stem that ends in a vowel (as in 배울 거예요 "will learn"). For the ㄹ-irregular verbs, -거예요 is used (as in 살 거예요 "will live").

A stem ending in a consonant:

스파게티를 먹을 거예요 "(I) will (probably) eat spaghetti"
오늘 밤 한국으로 떠날 거예요 "(I) will (probably) leave for Korea tonight"
내일 돈을 받을 거예요 "(I) will (probably) receive money tomorrow"

A stem ending in a vowel:

코미디 영화를 볼 거예요 "(I) will (probably) see a comedy movie"
일을 일찍 마칠 거예요 "(I) will (probably) end (my) work early"
내일 일찍 일어날 거예요 "(I) will (probably) get up early tomorrow"

A stem ending in a ㄹ-irregular:

아파트에서 살 거예요 "(I) will (probably) live in an apartment"
케이크를 만들 거예요 "(I) will (probably) make cakes"
친구 집에서 잘 거예요 "(I) will (probably) sleep at a friend's house"

The English "will" can sometimes indicate a speaker's intention in addition to the future event, as in "I will study hard." In a similar manner, -(으)ㄹ 거예요 can also indicate the intention of the speaker in addition to the future probability depending on the context. This is particularly true when the subject of the sentence is the first person. Consider the following examples:

저도 내일 학교에 갈 거예요 "I will also go to school tomorrow"
매일 운동 할 거예요 "(I) will exercise everyday"
꼭 돈을 받을 거예요 "Surely, (I) will receive the money"

When the subject is not the first or second person, the -(으)ㄹ 거예요 ending can indicate the speaker's conjecture. Consider the following examples:

내일은 눈이 올 거예요 "As for tomorrow, (I guess) snow may fall"
수잔은 오늘 밤 바쁠 거예요 "(I guess) as for Susan, (she) may be busy tonight"
한국은 더울 거예요 "(I guess) as for Korea, (it) may be hot"
시험이 어려울 거예요 "(I guess) the test may be difficult"
집 값이 비쌀 거예요 "(I guess) the housing price may be expensive"

When -(으)ㄹ 거예요 is used with the copula 이다, the ending indicates a probable present. For instance, consider the following sentences:

에린은 한국사람일 거예요 "Erin is probably a Korean"
그 차가 수잔 거일 거예요 "That car is probably Susan's"
도착지가 시카고일 거예요 "The destination is probably Chicago"

Indicating a wondering mindset and/or asking someone's opinion: -(으)ㄹ까요?

The -(으)ㄹ까? ending is used to indicate a speaker's wondering mindset and/or to seek the listener's opinion. To make the ending polite one can add 요 to the ending, as in -(으)ㄹ까요? The ending -(으)ㄹ까요? is a three form verb ending: -을까요? is used with the stem that ends in a consonant as in 먹을까요? and ㄹ까? is used with the stem that ends in a vowel as in 갈까요? With the ㄹ-irregular predicates, -까요? is used, as in 알까요?

When the speaker is (or part of) the subject, the -(으)ㄹ까요? ending expresses the speaker's wondering mindset. Consider the following sentences.

이번 주말에 어디로 <u>갈까요</u>? "(I) wonder where (I/we) should go this weekend"

어느 극장에서 <u>볼까요</u>? "(I) wonder at which theatre (I/we) should see (it)"

저녁은 무엇을 <u>먹을까요</u>? "As for dinner, (I) wonder what (I/we) shall eat"

언제 쯤 편지를 <u>받을까요</u>? "(I) wonder about when (I/we) should receive the letter"

저녁은 뭘 <u>만들까요</u>? "As for dinner, (I) wonder what (I/we) should make"

어느 신호등에서 <u>돌까요</u>? "(I) wonder at which traffic light (I/we) should make a turn"

Notice that the speaker is the subject of the sentence in the above examples. When the subject of the sentence is a third person, the -(으)ㄹ까요? ending is used to seek the listener's opinion. Consider the following sentences:

수잔이 어느 대학을 <u>갈까요</u>? "Which university do you think Susan will go?"

이 반지는 너무 <u>비쌀까요</u>? "As for this ring, do you think (it) will be too expensive?"

사무엘이 집에 <u>있을까요</u>? "Do you think that Samuel will be at home?"

제이야기를 <u>믿을까요</u>? "Do you think that (he) will believe my story?"

존이 어디서 <u>살까요</u>? "Where do you think John will live?"

토마스가 가게를 <u>열까요</u>? "Do you think that Thomas will open the store?"

The -(으)ㄹ까요? ending can be used for the past tense as well. Consider the following sentences:

폴이 결국 차를 샀을까요? "Do you think that Paul finally bought the car?"
앤드류가 한국에서 돌아왔을까요? "Do you think that Andrew returned from Korea?"

The repeated use of -(으)ㄹ까요? can be used to express alternative questions. For instance, consider the following sentences:

한국 음식을 먹을까요? 중국 음식을 먹을까요? "Shall (I/we) eat Korean food or Chinese food?"
코미디 영화를 볼까요? 로맨틱 영화를 볼까요? "Shall (I/we) see a comedy or romantic movie?"
집으로 갈까요? 도서관으로 갈까요? "Shall (I/we) go home or to the library?"

Notice that while the predicate (e.g., shall (I/we) eat ...) is used only once in English, the predicate is repeated in Korean.

Meanwhile, when -(으)ㄹ까요? is used with other verbs such as 하다 "do" and 생각하다 "think," it expresses the speaker's provisional idea regarding what s/he may do, corresponding to "I am thinking of doing something" in English. Consider the following sentences:

저도 한국에 갈까 해요. "I am also thinking of going to Korea."
저녁을 6 시에 먹을까 해요. "(I) am thinking of having dinner at 6 o'clock."
다음 학기에 한국어를 배울까 생각해요. "(I) am thinking of learning Korean next semester."

Exercises

Key vocabulary for Unit 21 exercises

가다 to go
가수 singer
가르치다 to teach
간호사 nurse
거리 road/street
공항 airport
그만두다 to quit
기자 journalist

기차 train
깨끗하다 to be clean
날씨 weather
놀다 to play

다음 next
대학교 university
덥다 to be hot (weather)
돕다 to help
듣다 to listen
마시다 to drink
맛있다 to be delicious
목수 carpenter
믿다 to believe
바쁘다 to be busy
방 room
배우 actor
배우다 to learn
백화점 department store
붐비다 to be congested
비싸다 to be expensive

사다 to buy
살다 to live
생일 birthday
아침 morning
약사 pharmacist
옷 clothes
요리하다 to cook
오늘 today
오다 to come
의사 medical doctor
음식 food
일 work
일본 Japan
자다 to sleep
전화하다 to make a phone call
조용하다 to be quiet
좋아하다 to like
주 week
집 house
축구 soccer
춥다 to be cold (weather)
친구들 friends
타다 to ride

한국어 the Korean language
형 older brother
화장품 cosmetics
회사원 office worker
흐리다 to be cloudy (weather)

Exercise 21.1

With the words below construct Korean sentences, using -(으)ㄹ 거예요.

Example: 토마스, 사과, 먹다
= 토마스는 사과를 먹을 거예요

 1 저, 야구, 하다
 2 저, 피아노, 치다
 3 우리, 태권도, 배우다
 4 줄리, 에어로빅, 하다
 5 리사, 일, 끝내다
 6 킴벌리, 학교 운동장, 뛰다
 7 사라, 집, 있다
 8 데이빗, 친구, 기다리다
 9 로렌, 물, 끓이다
10 폴, 돈, 모으다

Exercise 21.2

Change each sentence with -(으)ㄹ 거예요 and translate the sentence, as shown below:

Example: 학교에 가요
= 학교에 갈거예요 "(I) will (probably) go to school"

 1 공항에서 택시를 타요.
 2 한국어를 가르쳐요.
 3 다음 주에 일을 그만둬요.
 4 친구들이랑 집에서 놀아요.
 5 형의 말을 믿어요.
 6 친구의 생일 파티에 가요.
 7 내일 날씨는 추워요.
 8 아침에 조깅 해요.
 9 제이슨은 바빠요.
10 화장품을 사요.

Exercise 21.3

Write the dictionary form of the following irregular verbs below (refer to Unit 19 for irregular predicates).

>   Example: 날씨가 추울 거예요
>   = 춥다

     1 한국에서 살거예요.
     2 한국 노래를 들을 거예요.
     3 김치가 매울 거예요.
     4 친구를 도울 거예요.
     5 병이 나을 거예요.
     6 하늘이 파랄 거예요.
     7 노래를 부를 거예요.
     8 그 사실을 알거예요.
     9 돈을 벌 거예요.
    10 배가 고플 거예요.

Exercise 21.4

Change each sentence with -(으)ㄹ 거예요 and translate the sentence.

Example: 존이 미국 사람이에요
          = 존이 미국 사람일 거예요 "John is probably an American"

     1 일레인이 가수예요.
     2 찰스가 엔지니어예요.
     3 리디아가 의사예요.
     4 제이슨이 기자예요.
     5 엔지가 약사예요.
     6 브라이언이 회사원이예요.
     7 줄리가 간호사예요.
     8 사이몬이 목수예요.
     9 이사벨이 앵커우먼이에요.
    10 톰이 배우예요.

Exercise 21.5

Translate the following Korean sentences into English:

Example: 우리 한국에 갈까요?
= "Shall we go to Korea?"

1 제가 빵을 살까요?
2 제가 이 방에서 잘까요?
3 제가 요리할까요?
4 저희가 택시를 탈까요?
5 저희가 그 친구를 도울까요?
6 날씨가 흐릴까요?
7 음식이 맛있을까요?
8 옷이 비쌀까요?
9 에릭이 태권도를 배울까요?
10 제시카가 뉴욕에 올까요?

Exercise 21.6

Change each sentence with -(으)ㄹ까요? Then, translate the sentence as shown below:

Example: 브래드가 자전거를 타요
= 브래드가 자전거를 탈까요? "Do (you) think that Brad will ride a bicycle?"

1 선생님이 재즈를 들어요.
2 애니가 일본 차를 좋아해요.
3 제임스가 축구를 해요.
4 앨리스가 전화해요.
5 로렌스가 기차를 타요.
6 글렌이 와인을 마셔요.
7 집이 조용해요.
8 백화점이 붐벼요.
9 날씨가 더워요.
10 거리가 깨끗해요.

UNIT 22
Prenouns

Linguistic elements whose primary function is to modify the target noun are called "modifiers." Modifiers in Korean include prenouns, adjectives, and relative clauses. The focus of this unit is on prenouns. The sole function of prenouns is to modify and/or delimit the meaning of the nouns that they follow.

There are four groups of prenouns in Korean. The first group of prenouns are those that specifically delimit the quality or status of certain nouns. Consider the following example:

옛 이야기   "Old story"

Notice that 옛 "old" is a prenoun that delimits the quality or status of the noun 이야기 "story."

옛 "old" appears to be an adjective. However, prenouns differ from adjectives. A chief distinction between prenouns and adjectives is whether they are subject to morphological variations. Prenouns are nouns and they are not subject to any inflectional variation. On the other hand, adjectives are subject to variations. For example, in Korean, "a different school" can be written with a prenoun 딴 "another," or with an adjective 다른 "different."

딴 학교   (딴 "another" + 학교 "school")
다른 학교   (다른 "different" + 학교 "school")

Notice that 다른 is the conjugated form of 다르다 "to be different" (다르 + ㄴ = 다른). How to change an adjective stem into a noun-modifying form will be discussed in detail in the intermediate Korean. Here are some more examples of prenouns.

옛 말   "old saying" (옛 "old" + 말 "word")
옛 날   "old day" (옛 "old" + 날 "day")
옛 생각   "old memory" (옛 "old" + 생각 "thought")

새 노래	"new song" (새 "new" + 노래 "song")
새 학기	"new semester" (새 "new" + 학기 "semester")
새 신발	"new shoes" (새 "new" + 신발 "shoes")
헌 신발	"used shoes" (헌 "used" + 신발 "shoes")
헌 자동차	"used cars" (헌 "used" + 자동차 "cars")
헌 옷	"used clothes" (헌 "used" + 옷 "clothes")
맨 처음	"at the very first" (맨 "the very" + 처음 "first")
맨 앞	"at the very front" (맨 "the very" + 앞 "front")
맨 꼭대기	"the highest" (맨 "the very" + 꼭대기 "top")
딴 방법	"another method" (딴 "another" + 방법 "method")
딴 날	"some other day" (딴 "another" + 날 "day")
딴 사람	"different person" (딴 "another" + 사람 "person")
순 이익	"net profit" (순 "pure" + 이익 "profit")
순 모	"pure wool" (순 "pure" + 모 "wool")
순 한국식	"pure Korean style" (순 "pure" + 한국식 "Korean style")

Numbers

The second group of prenouns are numbers. Consider the following examples:

한 사람	"One person"
두 사람	"Two people"
열 사람	"Ten people"
한 살	"One year old"
두 살	"Two year old"
세 살	"Three year old"
일 층	"The first floor"
이 층	"The second floor"
삼 층	"The third floor"
일 학기	"The semester one"
이 학기	"The semester two"
삼 학기	"The semester three"

Notice that these numbers come before the noun (or counters) that they modify.

Demonstratives

The third group of prenouns includes demonstratives. Appearing before a noun that they modify, demonstratives indicate the speaker's physical as well as psychological distance relative to the listener or a referent. English has two demonstratives "this" and "that." However, Koreans make three referential locations: 이 "this (near the speaker)," 그 "that (near the listener)," and 저 "that over there (away from both the speaker and the listener)."

이 친구	"this friend"
그 친구	"that friend"
저 친구	"that friend (over there)"

Differing from English demonstratives, which can be used independently, as in "I like this," the Korean demonstratives cannot be used alone and must be followed by a noun. In other words, Korean demonstratives are always used with nouns, as in 이 친구 "this friend," 이 책 "this book," and so on.

Meanwhile, Korean has two dependent nouns that are often used with the demonstratives: 것 (or 거 in colloquial situations) "thing," and 곳 "place."

이 것 (or 이 거 for colloquial usages) "this (thing)"
그 것 (or 그 거 for colloquial usages) "that (thing)"
저 것 (or 저 거 for colloquial usages) "that (thing over there)"

이 곳 (or 여기 for colloquial usages) "here"
그 곳 (or 거기 for colloquial usages) "there"
저 곳 (or 저기 for colloquial usages) "over there"

Since 것 or 거 are dependent nouns which cannot be used by themselves, they are always used with a modifier (e.g., a prenoun, or an adjective).

Question prenouns

The fourth group includes question prenouns such as 어느 "which," and 무슨 (or 어떤) "what kind of."

무슨 음악을 좋아하세요? "What kind of music (do you) like?"
어떤 사람을 만나고 싶어요? "What kind of person (do you) wish to meet?"
어느 은행에 가세요? "Which bank (do you) go to?"

Notice that these question prenouns cannot be used by themselves, and they modify the nouns that they appear after.

Exercises

Key vocabulary for Unit 22 exercises

가다 to go
교수님 professor
교통 수단 transportation means
기다리다 to wait
나라 country
농구 basketball
듣다 to listen
만나다 to meet
백화점 department store
색 color
생일 birthday
선물 present
시계 watch
신문 newspaper
야구 baseball
여행하다 to travel
영화 movie
오다 to come
운동 sport/exercise
음식 food
음악 music
이용하다 to use
자주 often
장미 rose
좋아하다 to like
중국 China
지하철 subway
집 house
커피숍 coffee shop

Exercise 22.1

Underline whether the following statements are True or False.

Example: Prenouns modify the meanings of the nouns that they follow
(**T** / F)

1 The prenouns are not subject to morphological variations. (T / F)
2 Numbers are not prenouns. (T / F)
3 Just like English, Korean has two demonstratives. (T / F)
4 Korean demonstratives cannot be used independently. (T / F)
5 Certain question words are also prenouns in Korean. (T / F)

Exercise 22.2

Choose one of the prenouns from the list below to match the English translation.

List: 옛, 새, 헌, 맨, 딴, 순

Example: _____ 글 "ancient writing"
= 옛

1 _____ 집 "new house"
2 _____ 가방 "used bag"
3 _____ 생각 "another idea"
4 _____ 나중 "at the very end"
5 _____ 친구 "old friend"
6 _____ 것 "new thing"
7 _____ 책 "used book"
8 _____ 맛 "different taste"
9 _____ 왼쪽 "far left"
10 _____ 서울내기 "trueborn Seoulite"

Exercise 22.3

Fill in the blank with the appropriate expression.

Example: _____ (this book) 은 누구 거예요?
= 이 책

1 _____ (that house over there) 이 우리 집이에요.
2 _____ (this time) 을 기다렸어요.
3 _____ (that coffee shop over three) 에서 만나요.
4 _____ (this color) 를 좋아해요.
5 _____ (that professor) 은 한국 사람이에요.
6 _____ (this thing) 은 무엇입니까?
7 _____ (that thing) 은 신문이에요.
8 _____ (here) 로 오세요.
9 _____ (there) 에 가고 싶어요.
10 _____ (over there) 에서 만나요.

Exercise 22.4

Fill in the blank with the appropriate question prenoun (e.g., choose from 어느 or 무슨).

Example: A: _____ 음악을 좋아하세요?   B: R&B 를 좋아혜요
= 무슨

1 A: ____ 영화를 좋아하세요?   B: 액션 영화를 좋아해요.
2 A: ____ 나라 음식을 좋아하세요?   B: 중국 음식을 좋아해요.
3 A: ____ 교통 수단을 이용하세요?   B: 지하철을 이용해요.
4 A: ____ 생일 선물이 좋을까요?   B: 시계가 좋겠어요.
5 A: ____ 음악을 자주 들으세요?   B: 클래식을 좋아해요.
6 A: ____ 백화점에 가세요?   B: Sears 에 가요.
7 A: ____ 나라를 여행하고 싶으세요?   B: 스위스를 여행하고 싶어요.
8 A: ____ 운동을 좋아하세요?   B: 농구를 좋아해요.

UNIT 23
Adverbs and adverbials

The primary function of adverbs is to modify verbs and/or adjectives. Consider the following examples:

1 <u>일찍</u> 일어났어요. "(I) got up early."
2 <u>아마</u> 오늘 밤에 도착할 거예요. "Maybe, (he) will arrive tonight."
3 <u>매우</u> 맛있어요. "(It) is very delicious."
4 국이 <u>약간</u> 짜요. "The soup is a little salty."

In 1, 일찍 "early" modifies the verb 일어났어요 "got up," and 아마 "maybe" modifies the verb 도착할 거예요 "will arrive" in 2. In 3, 매우 "very" modifies the adjective 맛있어요 "delicious," and 약간 "little" modifies the adjective 짜요 "salty" in 4.

Three types of adverbs

Korean adverbs can be grouped into three types: sentential adverbs, conjunctional adverbs, and componential adverbs. Sentential adverbs modify a whole sentence. Conjunctional adverbs are those that connect two different sentences. Componential adverbs modify a specific part of the sentence such as verbs or adjectives. Consider the following sentences:

<u>하여튼</u> 커피가 <u>아주</u> 뜨거웠어요. <u>그리고</u> 비쌌어요
"Anyway, the coffee was very hot. And (it) was expensive"

하여튼 "anyway" is a sentential adverb since it modifies the entire sentence, 커피가 아주 뜨거웠어요 "the coffee was very hot." 아주 "very" is a componential adverb since it specifically modifies the adjective 뜨거웠어요 "was hot." 그리고 "and" is a conjunctional adverb since it connects two sentences.

Examples of sentential adverbs include the following:

가령 if/supposing
설령 even if
아마 perhaps
반드시 certainly

만일 if
설마 surely (not)
하여튼 anyway

Examples of conjunctional adverbs include:

그러나 but
그러니까 therefore
그러므로 since it is so
그렇지만 however
또 also
또는 or
따라서 accordingly
더군다나 besides

그리고 and
그래서 so
그런데 by the way
그럼 if so
또한 moreover
혹은 or
즉 in other words
더우기 moreover

There are three groups of componential adverbs depending on what kind of relation they modify, such as manner, temporal relations, and degree. First, manner adverbs express some relation of manner, for example:

빨리 fast/early/soon
멀리 far
매우 very/exceedingly
가장 most
너무 too much
혼자서 alone
많이 much
안녕히 at peace

천천히 slowly
가까이 shortly/nearly
제일 the first
아주 quite/very (much)
잘 well/often
함께 together
열심히 diligently

Time adverbs that concern temporal relations include the following:

막 just at the moment
벌써 long ago
아직 yet/still
요즈음 recently
현재 present
내일 tomorrow
갑자기 suddenly
당분간 for a while
줄곧 all the time
마침내 at last
언제나 all the time
늘 always
보통 usually

방금 right now
아까 some time ago
이미 already
지금 now
이따 later
모래 the day after tomorrow
냉큼 immediately
밤낮 night and day
드디어 finally
먼저 ahead
일찍 early
항상 at all times
가끔 sometimes

Degree adverbs include the following:

참 really   조금 a bit
주로 mainly   너무 so much
아주 very

However, when there is more than one componential adverb in a sentence, the adverbs tend to occur in the following sequence: time, degree, and manner, as shown below.

스티브가 항상 커피를 아주 많이 마셔요 "Steve <u>always</u> drinks coffee <u>very</u> <u>much</u>"

Notice that the first adverb is time adverb 항상 "always," followed by the degree adverb 아주 "very," and the manner adverb 많이 "much."

Adverbials

In Korean, adverbs do not take any morphological variation. Those adverbs that take morphological variations are called "adverbial." Consider the following examples:

1 점심을 맛있게 먹었어요. "(I) ate lunch deliciously."
2 꽃이 아름답게 피어요. "Flowers blossom beautifully."

In 1, notice that 맛있게 "deliciously" modifies the verb 먹었어요 "ate," and 아름답게 "beautifully" modifies 피어요 "blossom" in 2. However, 맛있게 or 아름답게 are not adverbs but adverbials in Korean, since they are the results of the morphological variations:

맛있다 "delicious"   : 맛있게 "deliciously" = 맛있 + 게
아름답다 "beautiful" : 아름답게 "beautifully" = 아름답 + 게

Notice above that the adverbial form -게 is attached to the adjective stems. In Korean, one can change an adjective into an adverbial form by attaching 게 to an adjective stem. Here are some more examples:

Adjectives   *Adverbials*
쉽다 easy   쉽게 easily
싸다 cheap   싸게 at a low price
크다 big   크게 hugely
작다 small   작게 tinily
넓다 wide   넓게 widely

싱겁다 mild (taste)   싱겁게 insipidly
행복하다 happy   행복하게 happily
간단하다 simple   간단하게 simply

Exercises

Key vocabulary for Unit 23 exercises

값 price
경치 scenery
공부하다 to study
궁금하다 to be curious
귤 tangerine
길 road
내일 tomorrow
느리다 to be slow
도서관 library

많이 much/a lot
맛없다 to be tasteless
맵다 to be spicy
머리 head
먹다 to eat
배우다 to learn
복잡하다 to be complex
부드럽다 to be soft/to be tender
쉽다 to be easy
시간 time
시원하다 to be cool/to be refreshing
시험 test
싸다 to be cheap
씩씩하다 to be manly

아름답다 to be beautiful
아프다 to be painful
연락 contact
오늘 today
외롭다 to be lonely
우습다 to be funny/to be laughable
위험하다 to be dangerous
유명하다 to be famous
음식 food
자다 to sleep

작다 to be small
전화 telephone
지하철 subway
주다 to give
타다 to ride
피곤하다 to be tired

Exercise 23.1

Fill in the blank with an appropriate manner adverb from the list below:

빨리, 천천히, 가까이, 매우, 가장, 너무, 잘 , 혼자서, 함께, 많이,
열심히

Example: 기사 아저씨, _____ 가 주세요 "Driver, please go quickly"
= 빨리

1 _____ 먹어요. "Eat slowly."
2 음식이 _____ 맛있어요. "The food is very delicious."
3 이 가게에서 이 옷이 _____ 비싸요 "This dress is the most expensive in this store."
4 _____ 많이 마시지 마세요. "Don't drink too much."
5 _____ 공부했어요. "(I) studied diligently."
6 우리 _____ 가요. "Let us go together."
7 _____ 사세요. "Buy much."
8 제니퍼가 _____ 만들었어요. "Jennifer made (it) by herself."
9 운동을 _____ 해요? "(Do you) play sports well?"
10 창문 옆에 _____ 앉으세요. "Sit closely to the window side."

Exercise 23.2

Fill in the blank with an appropriate time adverb from the list below:

내일, 막, 벌써, 아까 , 아직, 이미, 요즈음, 이따, 갑자기, 당분간,
밤낮, 드디어, 보통

Example: _____ 피터를 만날 거예요 "(I) will meet Peter tomorrow"
= 내일

1 지금 _____ 잡았어요. "(We) just caught (it) just at the moment."
2 _____ 저녁을 집에서 먹어요. "(I) usually eat dinner at home."

3 존이 _____ 집을 샀어요. "John bought the house long ago."
4 _____ 영화가 끝났어요. "The movie ended already."
5 _____ 서울에 도착했어요. "(We) finally arrived in Seoul."
6 _____ 컴퓨터 게임만 해요. "(I) play computer games night and day."
7 그럼 _____ 만나요. "Then see (you) later."
8 _____ 집에 있을 거예요. "(I) will be home for a while."
9 _____ 비가 와요. "The rain falls suddenly."
10 _____ 어떻게 지내세요? "How are (you) recently?"
11 편지가 _____ 안 왔어요. "The letter did not come yet."
12 찰스를 _____ 학교에서 만났어요. "(I) met Charles some time ago at school."

Exercise 23.3

Choose an appropriate conjunctional adverb from the list below:

그러나, 그리고, 그래서, 그러니까, 그런데, 그렇지만, 그럼

Example: 나는 아침을 안 먹어요. _____(however) 점심을 일찍
먹어요
= 그렇지만

1 내일 시험이 있어요. _____ (so) 오늘은 도서관에서 공부할 거예요.
2 한국에 가고 싶어요. _____ (however) 시간이 없어서 못 가요.
3 스테이크를 먹어요. _____(by the way) 어디서 먹을 거예요?
4 전화로 연락 주세요._____ (then) 안녕히 계세요.
5 머리가 아파요. _____ (so) 아스피린을 먹었어요.
6 어제 많이 못 잤어요. _____ (however) 안 피곤해요.
7 제주도는 경치가 아름다워요._____ (and) 귤로 유명해요.
8 한국어를 배우고 싶어요._____ (so) 서울에 가요.
9 음식 값이 싸요. _____ (but) 맛없어요.
10 길이 복잡해요._____ (therefore) 지하철을 타세요.

Exercise 23.4

Change the following adjectives into adverbials. Then translate the adverbials.

    Example: 아름답다
                = 아름답게 "beautifully"

 1 외롭다
 2 위험하다
 3 우습다
 4 쉽다
 5 시원하다
 6 씩씩하다
 7 부드럽다
 8 느리다
 9 궁금하다
10 맵다

UNIT 24

The endings -(으)ㄹ래요 -*(ŭ)l laeyo*
and -(으)ㄹ게요 -*(ŭ)lgeyo*

The -(으)ㄹ래요 ending "intention"

The -(으)ㄹ래요 ending indicates the speaker's intention or immediate desire, and it corresponds to "will" or "intend to" in English. The ending is used only with the verbs not with the adjectives, and it is normally used in colloquial settings.

The -(으)ㄹ래요 ending is a three-form ending: -을래요 is used after a stem that ends in a consonant, as in 먹을래요; -ㄹ래요 is used after a stem that ends in a vowel, as in 갈래요; -래요 is used for a ㄹ-irregular, as in 만들래요.

The -(으)ㄹ래요 ending is only used for the first person and the second person subjects. Consider the following conversation:

A: 뭐 시킬래요? "What will (you) order?"
B: 스테이크 먹을래요. "(I) will (intend to) eat steak."

As seen above, the -(으)ㄹ래요 ending is used in the second person question (for the first sentence) and the first person statement (in the second sentence). Here are some more examples:

A: 뭐 마실래요? "What will (you) drink?"
B: 커피 주세요. "Coffee please."

A: 어디로 갈래요? "Where will (you) go?"
B: 도서관에 갈래요. "(I) will go to the library."

The -(으)ㄹ래요 ending cannot be used for the third person subject, since one cannot speak for the third person's intention. Consequently, a sentence like 수잔이 커피 마실래요 is ungrammatical in Korean.

-(으)ㄹ래요 vs. -고 싶어요/싶어해요

The difference between -(으)ㄹ래요 and -고 싶어요/-고 싶어해요 is that while the former expresses an intention, the latter expresses a wish or hope. For instance, consider the following sentences:

오늘 스시를 먹을래요 "(I) will (intend) to eat Sushi today"
오늘 스시를 먹고 싶어요 "(I) want to eat Sushi today"

한국을 여행할래요 "(I) will (intend) to travel Korea"
한국을 여행하고 싶어요 "(I) want to travel Korea"

런던에 갈래요 "(I) will (intend) to go to London"
런던에 가고 싶어요 "(I) want to go to London"

As seen above, the sentences with the -고 싶어요 ending simply indicate the speaker's wish. However, the sentences with the -(으)ㄹ래요 ending indicate that the speaker has already made up his/her mind and will do so.

-(으)ㄹ래요 vs. -(으)ㄹ 거예요

In the previous unit, the -(으)ㄹ 거예요 ending that expresses the probable future as well as the first person speaker's intention was introduced. -(으)ㄹ 거예요 and -(으)ㄹ래요 can both be used to indicate the intention of the first person speaker, as shown below:

도서관에서 <u>만날 거예요</u> "(I) will meet (them) at the library"
도서관에서 <u>만날래요</u> "(I) will meet (them) at the library"

The meanings of both sentences are similar, and they can be used interchangeably. However, note that the usage of -(으)ㄹ 거예요 is much wider than that of -(으)ㄹ래요, in that -(으)ㄹ 거예요 can be used for the third person subject as well. When the speaker is not the first or second person, -(으)ㄹ 거예요 indicates the speaker's conjecture (refer to Unit 21 for review).

The -(으)ㄹ게요 ending "willingness"

The -(으)ㄹ게요 ending indicates the speaker's promise or willingness to do something for the listener's interest. The ending is used only for first person subject and only with the verbs not with the adjectives. Consider the following sentences:

A: 몇 시에 도서관에 올 거예요? "What time will (you) come to the library?"
B: 오전 9 시까지 <u>갈게요</u>. "(I) will (promise to) go (there) by 9 a.m."

Notice that speaker A asks what time B will come to the library. Speaker B's reply with (으)ㄹ게요 conveys a sense of promise or reassuring of "arriving at the library by 9 a.m." for speaker A's sake.

The -(으)ㄹ게요 ending is a three form ending: -을게요 is used after a stem that ends in a consonant, as in 먹을게요; -ㄹ게요 is used after a stem that ends in a vowel, as in 갈게요; -게요 is used for ㄹ-irregular verbs, as in 살게요 or 만들게요.

The -(으)ㄹ래요 ending and the -(으)ㄹ게요 ending seem to resemble each other since they can both be translated as "will" in English. However, there are two clear differences. First, while -(으)ㄹ래요 can be used for a second person in questions, -(으)ㄹ게요 cannot. This is because the -(으)ㄹ게요 ending is used only for the first person subject.

The second difference is that while -(으)ㄹ래요 indicates the speaker's intention, -(으)ㄹ게요 carries the speaker's sense of promise. Here are some examples for comparison.

열심히 공부할래요 "(I) will (intend to) study hard"
열심히 공부할게요 "(I) will (promise to) study hard"

몇 시에 집에 갈래요? "What time will (you intend to) go home?"
몇 시에 집에 갈게요? (X)

As -(으)ㄹ게요 conveys a sense of promise, it is often used when the speaker volunteers to do something. For instance, consider the following sentences.

공항에 제가 갈래요 "I will (intend to) go to the airport"
공항에 제가 갈게요 "I will (volunteer/promise to) go to the airport"

저녁은 제가 살래요 "As for dinner, I will (intend to) buy (it)"
저녁은 제가 살게요 "As for dinner, I will (volunteer/promise to) buy (it)"

Exercises

Key vocabulary for Unit 24 exercises

가다 to go
고르다 to choose
공부하다 to study
기다리다 to wait
꽃병 vase
내다 to pay
노래 song

누나 older sister
닫다 to close
도서관 library
돈 money
돕다 to help

만나다 to meet
만들다 to make
먹다 to eat
문 door
물 water
미국 USA
믿다 to believe
방학 vacation
밤 night
보다 to see
부르다 to sing/to call out
부엌 kitchen
부치다 to mail out

사귀다 to make friends
사다 to buy
살다 to live
색 color
손 hand
시키다 to order
씻다 to wash
아버지 father
아침 morning
열다 to open
영화 movie
오전 a.m.
오후 p.m.
이야기 story
일본 Japan
일어나다 to get up

자다 to sleep
전화하다 to make a phone call
주다 to give
즐기다 to enjoy
집 house
차 car
창문 window
친구 friend

팔다 to sell
편지 letter
학교 school
한국어 the Korean language

Exercise 24.1

Conjugate the verb with the -(으)ㄹ래요 ending. Then translate the sentence.

Example: 점심을 (먹다)
= 점심을 먹을래요 "(I) will (intend to) eat lunch"

1 한국 영화를 (보다).
2 일본 차를 (사다).
3 미국에서 (살다).
4 누나의 이야기를 (믿다).
5 친구를 (돕다).
6 손을 (씻다).
7 친구를 (기다리다).
8 꽃병에 물을 (주다).
9 방학을 (즐기다).
10 한국인 친구를 (사귀다).

Exercise 24.2

Answer the questions below using the information provided in brackets:

Example: "What time will you go home? (9 o'clock in the morning)"
= 아침 9 시에 갈래요

1 "Where will you (intend to) go? (home)"
2 "Where will you (intend to) live? (Boston)"
3 "What time will you (intend to) go to bed? (11 o'clock at night)"
4 "Where will you (intend to) study? (the library)"
5 "Where will you (intend to) make kimchi? (kitchen)"
6 "What will you (intend to) eat? (pasta)"
7 "What will you (intend to) see? (Korean movie)"
8 "What will you (intend to) learn? (the Korean language)"
9 "What time will you (intend to) get up? (6 o'clock in the morning)"
10 "Who will you (intend to) meet? (father)"

Exercise 24.3

Change the verb as in the example, and translate the sentence.

> Example: 제가 열쇠를 (찾다)
> = 제가 열쇠를 찾을게요 "I will (promise to) find the key"

 1 제가 차를 (팔다).
 2 제가 창문을 (열다).
 3 제가 노래를 (부르다).
 4 제가 샐러드 (시키다).
 5 제가 (돕다).
 6 제가 돈을 (내다).
 7 제가 학교에 (전화하다).
 8 제가 색을 (고르다).
 9 제가 편지를 (부치다).
10 제가 가게 문을 (닫다).

Exercise 24.4

Underline which of the two English translations below is the correct version of the Korean in each case:

> Example: 학교에 갈게요
> = "(I) will (intend to) go to school."/"(I) will (promise to) go to school"

 1 양복을 입을 거예요.
   "(I) will (promise to) wear a suit."/"(I) will (probably) wear a suit."
 2 친구한테 연락할게요.
   "(I) will (intend to) contact the friend."/"(I) will (promise to) contact the friend."
 3 제가 햄버거를 만들래요.
   "I will (intend to) make hamburgers."/"I will (promise to) make hamburgers."
 4 친구 집에서 잘 거예요.
   "(I) will (probably) sleep over the friend's house."/"(I) will (promise to) sleep over the friend's house."
 5 주말에 전화할게요.
   "(I) will (intend to) make a phone call this weekend."/"(I) will (promise to) make a phone call this weekend."
 6 일을 그만둘래요.
   "(I) will (intend to) quit the work."/"(I) will (probably) quit the work."

7 내일 일찍 일어날게요.
"(I) will (promise to) get up early tomorrow."/"(I) will (probably) get up early tomorrow."

8 앞 자리에 앉을래요.
"(I) will (intend to) sit in the front seat."/"(I) will (promise to) sit in the front seat."

9 선생님한테 말할 거예요.
"(I) will (probably) talk to the teacher."/"(I) will (promise to) talk to the teacher."

10 태권도를 배울래요.
"(I) will (intend to) learn Taekwondo."/"(I) will (promise to) learn Taekwondo."

UNIT 25
The suffixes -겠 -*ket* and -(으)시 -*(ŭ)si*

Inferential and intentional suffix -겠

The suffix 겠 is a pre-final ending that comes between the stem of the predicate and the final-ending (e.g., speech level), as in 하겠습니다 (하 + 겠 + 습니다) "will do." The suffix 겠 is used to indicate two things.

First, when the subject of the predicate is the first and/or second person, the suffix 겠 expresses the speaker's intention or asks the listener's intention, and it corresponds to "will" in English. It is used for first person statements and/or second person questions.

제가 내일 공항에 가겠습니다	"I will go to the airport tomorrow"
열심히 공부하겠습니다	"(I) will study hard"
스테이크를 주문하겠습니다	"(I) will order steak"
내일 오후 다시 오겠습니다	"(I) will come again tomorrow afternoon"
신용 카드로 지불하시겠습니까?	"Will (you) pay by a credit card?"
어디로 가시겠습니까?	"Where will (you) go?"

Notice that the meaning of the suffix 겠 is similar to -(으)ㄹ래요 "will." However, while -(으)ㄹ래요 is normally used in colloquial usages, the suffix 겠 is used for more formal usages.

Second, when the subject of the predicate is not either the first or second person (e.g., the third person or entity), the suffix 겠 indicates the speaker's conjecture or asks the listener's idea regarding the topic in question. It is corresponding to "I guess/think" (for the first person statement) or "do you think that . . ." (for the second person question) in English.

내일 시험이 어렵겠어요	"(I guess that) tomorrow's test will be difficult"
드라마가 재미있겠어요	"(I guess that) the drama will be interesting"
다리가 아팠겠어요	"(I guess that your) legs were sore"

학교 식당 커피가 맛있겠어요? "Do you think that the school cafeteria coffee is delicious?"
기름 값이 쌌겠어요? "Do you think that the price of oil was cheap?"

The suffix 겠 is used in formal or broadcasting contexts, such as weather forecasts and news reports. Consider the following examples.

오늘 밤부터 눈이 오겠습니다 "(I guess that) snow will fall (starting) from tonight"
내일은 춥겠습니다 "(I guess that) as for tomorrow, (it) will be cold"

The subject honorific suffix -(으)시

When Koreans wish to honor the subject of the sentence (e.g., who they are talking to or who they are talking about), they make a predicate form honorific by attaching the honorific suffix -(으)시 to the stem of the predicate. The honorific suffix -(으)시 is a pre-final ending that comes between the stem of the predicate and the final ending. -으시 is added after the stem that ends in a consonant, as in 찾으시다 (찾 + 으시 + 다) "look for," and 시 is added after a stem that ends in a vowel, as in 가시다 (가 + 시 + 다) "go."

Dictionary form	Polite speech level	Deferential speech level
가다 "go"	가요	갑니다
가시다 "go"	가세요	가십니다
	(가 + 시 + 어요)	(가 + 시 + ㅂ니다)
입다 "wear"	입어요	입습니다
입으시다 "wear"	입으세요	입으십니다
	(입 + 으시 + 어요)	(입 + 으시 + ㅂ니다)

Notice that although the referential meanings of the verbs 가다 and 가시다 (or 입다 and 입으시다) are the same, their social meanings are different. The presence of the honorific suffix indicates the speaker's attitude toward the subject of the sentence.

Various social variables that are ascribed (e.g., age, kinship relations) and/or achieved (e.g., occupation, seniority, rank) determine the honorific suffix usage. For instance, Koreans use the honorific suffix when they talk to or talk about their older family members, older people in general, people of esteemed occupations (e.g., doctors, lawyers, teachers, etc.), senior-rank personnel, and so forth.

The subject being honored can be either an addressee (to whom the speaker is talking) or a referent (who the speaker is talking about). Consider the following examples:

1 교수님, 어디에 가세요? "Where are (you) going, Professor?"
2 김 교수님이 오세요. "Professor Kim is coming."

Notice that in 1, the subject being honored is the addressee, whereas the subject of 2 is the third-person referent.

The use of different speech level endings is related to who you are talking to rather than who you are talking about. In other words, the choice of appropriate speech levels depends on the addressee not on the referent. However, since the honorific suffix honors the subject of the sentence (e.g., either an addressee or referent), the suffix can be used with any other speech levels. For instance, one of the Korean speech levels used to address a child or childhood-friend is the intimate speech level -어/아. Consider the following sentence:

어머니는 어디에 가서? "As for (your) mother, where does (she) go?"

Notice that the speaker uses the intimate speech level but honors the mother by using the suffix (e.g., 가셔 = 가 + 시 + 어).

The following Korean verbs that have the corresponding honorific forms, do not take the suffix to their stems.

먹다 "eat"   잡수시다 "eat (honorific)"
자다 "sleep"   주무시다 "sleep (honorific)"
있다 "exist/stay"   계시다 "exist/stay (honorific)"

However, notice that the suffix 시 is already part of these euphemistic verbs.

Meanwhile, Koreans do not use the honorific suffix when the subject of the sentence is the speaker himself or herself. In other words, one does not show honor toward him/herself. Consider the following samples:

A: 어디에 가세요? "Where are (you) going?"
B: 집에 가요. "(I) am going home."

Notice that speaker A uses the suffix when asking the question to B. However, speaker B does not use the suffix in the reply.

Exercises

Key vocabulary for Unit 25 exercises

가르치다 to teach
값 price

거실 living room
건너다 to cross (the road, bridge)
고등학교 high school
공부하다 to study
교통 traffic
금요일 Friday
기다리다 to wait
길 road
깨끗하다 to be clean
꼭 surely
끊다 to quit
날씨 weather
내리다 to fall/to drop
내일 tomorrow

담배 cigarette
덥다 to be hot (weather)
두드리다 to knock (door)
마치다 to finish
막히다 to be held up
많이 much/a lot
맛있다 to be delicious
매일 everyday
먹다 to eat
문 door
미끄럽다 to be slippery
믿다 to believe
바람 wind
방 room
보다 to see
불다 to blow
비 rain
비싸다 to be expensive
선생님 teacher
쉽다 to be easy
시험 test
약속 promise
어렵다 to be difficult
에어로빅 aerobics
열쇠 key
열심히 hard/earnestly
영화 movie
운동 sport/exercise

음식 food
일 work

자다 to sleep
재미있다 to be interesting
저녁 dinner
전화하다 to make a phone call
점심 lunch
조용하다 to be quiet
좁다 to be narrow
좋다 to be good
준비하다 to prepare
지키다 to keep
지하철 subway
집 house
찾다 to find
춥다 to be cold (weather)
치다 to play/to hit
친구 friend
타다 to ride
팔다 to sell
품질 quality
하다 to do
흐리다 to be cloudy

Exercise 25.1

Add 겠 to the predicate as in the example and translate the sentence.

 Example: 저는 집에 (가다)
       = 저는 집에 가겠습니다 "As for me, (I) will go home"

 1 제가 금요일까지 일을 (마치다).
 2 제가 매일 (운동하다).
 3 내일은 제가 지하철을 (타다).
 4 제가 저녁을 (준비하다).
 5 제가 친구를 (기다리다).
 6 시험이 (쉽다).
 7 내일 날씨가 (춥다).
 8 드라마가 (재미있다).
 9 집 값이 (비싸다).
10 품질이 (좋다).

Exercise 25.2

Translate the following into English:

> Example: 데니엘이 학교에 갔겠어요?
> = "(Do you think that) Daniel went to school?"

1 (the subject is the addressee) 담배를 끊겠습니까?
2 (the subject is the addressee) 열심히 공부하겠습니까?
3 집이 조용하겠습니까?
4 음식이 맛있겠습니까?
5 길이 좁겠습니까?
6 내일 날씨는 덥겠습니까?
7 방이 깨끗하겠습니까?
8 토마스가 버스를 탔겠습니까?
9 이사벨이 전화했겠습니까?
10 제시카가 친구를 기다렸겠습니까?

Exercise 25.3

Translate the following into Korean.

> Example: "(I) will jog everyday"
> = 매일 조깅 하겠습니다

1 "(I) will do aerobics everyday."
2 "Surely, (I) will keep the promise."
3 "Surely, (I) will find the key."
4 "Surely, (I) will quit smoking."
5 "Surely, (I) will sell the home."
6 "As for tomorrow, (I guess) it will be cloudy."
7 "As for tomorrow, (I guess) rain will fall."
8 "As for tomorrow, (I guess) wind will blow a lot."
9 "As for tomorrow, (I guess that) the traffic will be held up."
10 "As for tomorrow, (I guess that) the road will be slippery."

Exercise 25.4

Change the following verb into the honorific form using the honorific suffix -(으)시 and translate the sentence.

Example: 집에 (가다)
= 집에 가십니다 "(He) goes home"

1 길을 (건너다)
2 골프를 (치다)
3 한국어를 (가르치다)
4 문을 (두드리다)
5 한국 영화를 (보다)
6 그 친구를 (믿다)
7 고등학교 선생님 (이다)
8 점심을 (먹다)
9 거실에서 (자다)
10 학교에 (있다)

KEY TO EXERCISES

Unit 1

Exercises 1.1

다

Exercise 1.2

궈

Exercise 1.3

거

Exercise 1.4

과

Exercise 1.5

1 bus
2 coffee
3 coat
4 jazz
5 quiz
6 romance
7 taxi
8 Starbucks
9 hot dog
10 sandwich
11 hamburger
12 camera

Exercise 1.6

1　Brazil
2　Spain
3　Norway
4　Finland
5　Philippines
6　Italy
7　France
8　England
9　Canada
10　Mexico

Exercise 1.7

1　New York
2　Sydney
3　San Francisco
4　London
5　Paris
6　Seoul
7　Madrid
8　Las Vegas
9　New Delhi
10　Lisbon

Exercise 1.8

1　러시아
2　이집트
3　포르투갈
4　헝가리
5　사우디 아라비아
6　뉴질랜드
7　아르헨티나
8　인디아
9　오스트레일리아
10　이스라엘

Exercise 1.9

1　상하이
2　카이로
3　리오데 자네이로

  4 토쿄
  5 모스크바
  6 헬싱키
  7 로마
  8 오슬로
  9 방콕
 10 멕시코시티

Exercise 1.10

  1 Jimmy Carter
  2 George Bush
  3 Abraham Lincoln
  4 George Washington
  5 Winston Churchill
  6 Thomas Edison
  7 Bill Clinton
  8 Leonardo da Vinci
  9 Elvis Presley
 10 John Lennon

Exercise 1.11

  1 모니터
  2 샴푸
  3 피자
  4 스키
  5 텔레비전
  6 펜
  7 카드
  8 쿠키
  9 팝송
 10 나이프
 11 바나나
 12 오렌지

Unit 2

Exercise 2.1

  1 T   2 F   3 F   4 F   5 F
  6 T   7 T   8 T   9 T

Exercise 2.2

1 마이클이 운동장에서 조깅 해요.
2 조앤이 점심을 먹어요.
3 티모티가 농구를 해요.
4 브루스가 텔레비전을 봐요.
5 마크가 스파게티를 만들어요.
6 다이앤이 집에서 자요.
7 캐롤이 필립한테 이야기해요.
8 테디가 커피를 마셔요.
9 찰스가 학교에 가요.
10 토니가 피아노를 쳐요.

Exercise 2.3

1 2005, December 24
2 Kim Sumi
3 Republic of Korea, Kyonggi Province, Seoul, Jung District, Hankuk Street 712–19.
4 Lee Daesung
5 1977, May 18
6 Republic of Korea, Kyonggi Province, Seoul, Kangnam District, Taehan Street 81–3.

Unit 3

Exercise 3.1

1 bird	2 business	3 fan	4 wall	5 meat
6 egg	7 needle	8 rubber	9 herbs	10 music

Exercise 3.2

1	고무신	rubber shoes	= 고무 rubber	+ 신 shoes
2	산나물	wild edible greens	= 산 mountain	+ 나물 greens
3	벽돌	brick	= 벽 wall	+ 돌 stone
4	앞문	font door	= 앞 front	+ 문 door
5	코피	blood from the nose	= 코 nose	+ 피 blood
6	바닷가	the seaside	= 바다 sea	+ 가 side
7	빵집	bakery	= 빵 bread	+ 집 house
8	책방	bookstore	= 책 book	+ 방 room
9	물개	seal	= 물 water	+ 개 dog
10	철새	migratory bird	= 철 season	+ 새 bird

Exercise 3.3

1 Prefix: 신 Meaning: new
2 Prefix: 고 Meaning: high
3 Prefix: 불 Meaning: not

Exercise 3.4

1 Suffix: 식 Meaning: style
2 Suffix: 질 Meaning: (the act of) doing
3 Suffix: 직 Meaning: job

Unit 4

Exercise 4.1

1 Adjective 가볍
2 Verb 가지
3 Verb 팔
4 Verb 달
5 Adjective 많
6 Verb 만지
7 Verb 타
8 Verb 앉
9 Adjective 시
10 Adjective 넓

Exercise 4.2

The blunt and familiar speech levels.

Exercise 4.3

The deferential speech level.

Exercise 4.4

1 Deferential   묶습니다
2 Polite   묶어요
3 Intimate   묶어
4 Plain   묶는다

Exercise 4.5

1 Deferential   넣습니까
2 Polite   넣어요
3 Intimate   넣어
4 Plain   넣니

Exercise 4.6

1 Deferential   배웁시다
2 Polite   배워요
3 Intimate   배워
4 Plain   배우자

Exercise 4.7

1 Deferential   읽으십시오
2 Polite   읽어요
3 Intimate   읽어
4 Plain   읽어라

Unit 5

Exercise 5.1

1 점심을 먹습니다. "(I) eat lunch."
2 한국어를 가르칩니다. "(I) teach Korean."
3 친구를 기다립니다. "(I) wait for the friend."
4 커피를 마십니다. "(I) drink coffee."
5 편지를 받습니다. "(I) receive a letter."
6 영어를 배웁니다. "(I) learn English."
7 방이 깨끗합니다. "The room is clean."
8 기차가 느립니다. "The train is slow."
9 물이 뜨겁습니다. "The water is hot."
10 매일 바쁩니다. "(I) am busy everyday."

Exercise 5.2

1 언제 가게 문을 닫습니까? "When (do you) close the store door?"
2 어디서 손을 씻습니까? "Where (do you) wash your hand?"
3 언제 앉습니까? "When (do you) sit?"
4 어디서 잡니까? "Where (do you) sleep?"
5 담배를 피웁니까? "(Do you) smoke?"
6 지갑을 찾습니까? "(Do you) look for a wallet?"

7 날씨가 춥습니까? "Is the weather cold?"
8 시험이 쉽습니까? "Is the test easy?"
9 기분이 좋습니까? "Is your feeling good?"
10 집이 시끄럽습니까? "Is the house noisy?"

Exercise 5.3

1 길을 건너십시오. "Cross the street."
2 밑으로 내려가십시오. "Go down to the bottom."
3 공을 던지십시오. "Throw the ball."
4 문을 두드리십시오. "Knock on the door."
5 선생님을 따르십시오. "Follow the teacher."
6 친구를 믿으십시오. "Believe the friend."
7 구두를 신으십시오. "Wear the shoes."
8 코트를 입으십시오. "Wear the coat."
9 손을 잡으십시오. "Hold hands."
10 크게 외치십시오. "Shout aloud."

Exercise 5.4

1 편지를 보냅시다! "(Let us) send the letter!"
2 그림을 그립시다! "(Let us) draw a painting!"
3 물고기를 잡읍시다! "(Let us) catch fish!'
4 책을 읽읍시다! "(Let us) read the book!"
5 일을 마칩시다! "(Let us) finish the work!"
6 버스를 탑시다! "(Let us) take a bus!"
7 여기서 헤어집시다! "(Let us) depart here!"
8 코미디 영화를 봅시다! "(Let us) see a comedy movie!"
9 기회를 줍시다! "(Let us) give (them) a chance!"
10 쓰레기를 버립시다! "(Let us) throw away the garbage!"

Exercise 5.5

1 "Read page 5."
2 "(Let us) wash hands."
3 "Close the window."
4 "(Let us) borrow the book."
5 "Go out from the library."
6 "Drink water."
7 "(Let us) give (them) food."
8 "(Let us) wear the uniform."
9 "Learn the Korean language."
10 "(Let us) leave for Seoul."

Exercise 5.6

1 길을 건너요. "(I) cross the street."
2 문을 열어요. "(I) open the door."
3 책을 팔아요. "(I) sell the book."
4 쓰레기를 버려요. "(I) throw away the garbage."
5 문을 닫아요. "(I) close the door."
6 일을 마쳐요. "(I) finish the work."
7 책을 빌려요. "(I) borrow a book."
8 손을 씻어요. "(I) wash hands."
9 아침에 일찍 일어나요. "(I) get up early in the morning."
10 택시를 타요. "(I) ride a taxi."
11 집이 좋아요. "The house is good."
12 영화가 재미있어요. "The movie is interesting."
13 한국 사람이에요. "(I) am a Korean."
14 숙제를 해요. "(I) do homework."
15 대학생이 아니에요. "(I) am not a college student."
16 학교가 멀어요. "The school is far."
17 커피가 달아요. "The coffee is sweet."
18 배가 아파요. "My stomach hurts."
19 하늘이 흐려요. "The sky is cloudy."
20 야채가 싱싱해요. "The vegetables are fresh."

Unit 6

Exercise 6.1

1 토마스 (가) 있어요. "There is Thomas."
2 수잔 (이) 있어요. "There is Susan."
3 바바라 (가) 있어요. "There is Barbara."
4 앤드류 (가) 있어요. "There is Andrew."
5 폴 (이) 있어요. "There is Paul."
6 존 (이) 있어요. "There is John."
7 에비 (가) 있어요. "There is Abby."
8 앤서니 (가) 있어요. "There is Anthony."
9 캐서린 (이) 있어요. "There is Catherine."
10 찰스 (가) 있어요. "There is Charles."

Exercise 6.2

1 영화가 재미있습니다. "The movie is interesting."
2 한국 사람이 많습니다. "There are many Koreans."
3 음식이 맛없습니다. "The food is tasteless."
4 도서관이 조용합니다. "The library is quiet."

5 자동차가 비쌉니다. "The car is expensive."
6 학교가 가깝습니다. "The school is near."
7 성격이 좋습니다. "The personality is good."
8 음식이 짭니다. "The food is salty."

Exercise 6.3

1 "The school is far."
2 "The room is clean."
3 "The coffee is sweet."
4 "The Korean food is delicious."
5 "The price is cheap."

Exercise 6.4

1 "The house is big."
2 "The puppy is cute."
3 "The weather is hot."
4 "The test is difficult."
5 "The head is dizzy."

Exercise 6.5

1 스케줄이 짧아요.
2 펜이 비싸요.
3 집이 넓어요.
4 초콜릿이 달아요.
5 컴퓨터가 비싸요.

Exercise 6.6

1 날씨가 흐립니다.
2 길이 위험합니다.
3 시험이 쉽습니다.
4 방이 더럽습니다.
5 캠퍼스가 아름답습니다.

Exercise 6.7

1 일레인은 가수가 아니에요.
2 찰스는 엔지니어가 아니에요.
3 리디아는 의사가 아니에요.
4 제이슨은 기자가 아니에요.
5 엔지는 약사가 아니에요.

6 브라이언은 회사원이 아니에요.
7 줄리는 간호사가 아니에요.
8 사이몬은 목수가 아니에요.
9 이사벨은 앵커우먼이 아니에요.
10 톰은 영화 배우가 아니에요.

Exercise 6.8

1 초콜릿
2 설탕
3 약
4 국
5 음식
6 김치
7 커피
8 물
9 레몬
10 차

Unit 7

Exercise 7.1

1 유미꼬는 일본 사람이에요. "As for Yumiko, (she) is a Japanese."
2 캐서린은 캐나다 사람이에요. "As for Katherine, (she) is a Canadian."
3 왜이는 중국 사람이에요. "As for Wei, (she) is a Chinese."
4 혜진이는 한국 사람이에요. "As for Haejin, (she) is a Korean."
5 존은 영국 사람이에요. "As for John, (he) is a British."
6 스티브는 호주 사람이에요. "As for Steve, (he) is an Australian."
7 루이스는 프랑스 사람이에요. "As for Luis, (he) is a French."
8 마리오는 멕시코 사람이에요. "As for Mario, (he) is a Mexican."
9 이반은 러시아 사람이에요. "As for Ivan, (he) is a Russian."
10 알프레도는 이탈리아 사람이에요. "As for Alfredo, (he) is an Italian."

Exercise 7.2

1 음악은 재즈를 좋아해요. "As for music, (I) like jazz."
2 영화는 코미디를 좋아해요. "As for movie, (I) like comedy."
3 운동은 야구를 좋아해요. "As for sport, (I) like baseball."
4 책은 한국 소설을 좋아해요. "As for book, (I) like Korean novels."
5 꽃은 장미를 좋아해요. "As for flower, (I) like roses."
6 과목은 역사를 좋아해요. "As for subject, (I) like history."

7 계절은 봄을 좋아해요. "As for season, (I) like spring."
8 색은 파랑을 좋아해요. "As for color, (I) like blue."
9 컴퓨터는 맥켄토씨를 좋아해요. "As for computer, (I) like Macintosh."
10 자동차는 BMW 를 좋아해요. "As for car, (I) like BMW."

Exercise 7.3

1 애린은 캐나다에 있어요.
2 자슈아는 멕시코에 있어요.
3 플로렌스는 브라질에 있어요.
4 로날드는 필리핀에 있어요.
5 프랜시스는 뉴질랜드에 있어요.
6 윌리엄은 러시아에 있어요.
7 크리스틴은 프랑스에 있어요.
8 찰스는 이탈리아에 있어요.
9 사라는 중국에 있어요.
10 마이클은 일본에 있어요.

Exercise 7.4

1 누가 제임스예요?
2 색은 흰색을 좋아해요.
3 오늘 날씨는 더워요.
4 택시가 비싸요.
5 학교가 멀어요.
6 커피는 해이즐넛이 맛있어요.

Exercise 7.5

1 테렌스가 3 학년이에요.
2 스티븐은 1 학년이에요.
3 어디가 은행이에요?
4 상우가 한국 사람이에요.
5 켄은 일본 사람이에요.
6 마리오는 멕시코 사람이에요.
7 누가 선생님이에요?
8 자동차는 현대가 좋아요.
9 제 이름은 앤드류예요.
10 제 고향은 서울이에요.

Unit 8

Exercise 8.1

1 나   2 저   3 저   4 저희   5 우리
6 저희   7 나   8 나   9 나   10 나

Exercise 8.2

1 제 전공   2 내 컴퓨터   3 저희 가족   4 우리 누나
5 내 지갑   6 내 신발   7 제 사무실   8 제 가방
9 우리 아버지   10 저희 회사

Exercise 8.3

1 저기요   2 너   3 아버지   4 누나
5 할아버지   6 여보   7 형   8 너

Exercise 8.4

1 형   2 할아버지   3 어머니   4 여동생
5 아버지   6 선생님   7 그 사람   8 큰아버지

Exercise 8.5

1 M   2 F   3 F   4 M
5 M   6 F   7 F   8 F

Exercise 8.6

1 "My/our grandfather was a government employee."
2 "My/our father is an office worker."
3 "My/our mother is an elementary school teacher."
4 "My/our uncle is an engineer."
5 "My/our maternal grandfather is in Seoul."
6 "My/our maternal uncle is in New York."
7 "My/our older brother is a graduate student."
8 "My/our grandson is in Korea."

Unit 9

Exercise 9.1

1	18	6	17	11	24
2	9	7	63	12	92
3	41	8	75	13	230
4	81	9	56	14	67
5	1459	10	102	15	18,746

Exercise 9.2

1	7	6	23	11	90
2	18	7	33	12	72
3	25	8	11	13	48
4	17	9	64	14	56
5	87	10	49	15	22

Exercise 9.3

1	셋	6	열여덟	11	서른 둘
2	열여섯	7	스물	12	여든 일곱
3	마흔 다섯	8	쉰둘	13	열아홉
4	아흔 둘	9	서른	14	스물 넷
5	열하나	10	예순 셋	15	일흔 다섯

Exercise 9.4

1	육	6	십오	11	이십구
2	십일	7	백오십삼	12	십팔
3	삼십칠	8	육십일	13	삼백칠십이
4	사십이	9	칠십사	14	구십구
5	오백십칠	10	삼천이십일	15	오만 삼천이백칠십육

Exercise 9.5

1	제 팔/ 여덟 째	6	제 십오/ 열다섯 째
2	제 이십칠/ 스물 일곱 째	7	제 팔십육/ 여든 여섯 째
3	제 이/ 두 째	8	제 이십/ 스무 째
4	제 십삼/ 열세 째	9	제 이십사/ 스물 네 째
5	제 사십/ 마흔 째	10	제 십육/ 열여섯 째

Exercise 9.6

1 9 students	6 3 students
2 24 students	7 15 students
3 8 Koreans	8 16 Koreans
4 32 Koreans	9 158 Koreans
5 1452 Koreans	10 89 Koreans

Unit 10

Exercise 10.1

1 3 animals	6 5 pieces	11 10 times
2 4 hours	7 6 bottles	12 76 miles
3 1 kind	8 20 years (old)	13 359 dollars
4 13 items	9 24 books	14 18 months (duration)
5 36 couples	10 98 people	15 120 minutes

Exercise 10.2

1 일곱 병	6 두 군데	11 세 쌍
2 아홉 조각	7 열두 상자	12 한 봉지
3 열한 살	8 여덟 잔	13 구 월
4 사 층	9 십삼 개월	14 육십 초
5 삼십육 년	10 여섯 개	15 다섯 시간

Exercise 10.3

1 10:45 a.m.	6 09:32 a.m.
2 07:50 p.m.	7 06:18 p.m.
3 08:00 in the morning	8 10:09 in the morning
4 06:27 in the evening	9 07:30 in the evening
5 04:46 a.m.	10 05:34 p.m.

Exercise 10.4

1 오후 열한 시 십오 분	6 오전 여덟 시 육 분
2 오후 열 시 삼십 이 분	7 오전 여섯 시 이십삼 분
3 오전 열한 시 이십오 분	8 오후 여섯 시 이십팔 분
4 오후 두 시 삼십 분 (or 반)	9 오후 네 시 구 분
5 오전 세 시 사십팔 분	10 오전 다섯 시 오십일 분

Exercise 10.5

1 (일)천구백 사십삼 년 삼 월 십육 일
2 (일)천구백 칠십이 년 일 월 십팔 일
3 (일)천구백 육십오 년 십이 월 이십오 일
4 (일)천구백 오십구 년 이 월 십사 일
5 (일)천구백 칠십 년 오 월 칠 일
6 (일)천구백 구십사 년 구 월 삼십일 일
7 이천일 년 칠 월 사 일
8 이천육 년 십일 월 오 일
9 (일)천구백 삼십육 년 사 월 삼십 일
10 (일)천구백 구십팔 년 팔 월 십이 일

Exercise 10.6

1 4 Chinese people	6 6 tigers
2 5 cups of water	7 11 bikes
3 8 houses	8 9 volumes of novel
4 2 pairs of sneakers	9 6 roses
5 10 slices of a pizza	10 12 bottles of wine

Exercise 10.7

1 미국인 일곱 명	6 신발 두 켤레
2 장미 다섯 송이	7 커피 여덟 잔
3 한국어 책 열 권	8 맥주 아홉 병
4 자동차 세 대	9 일본인 네 명
5 나무 여섯 그루	10 개 스무 마리

Unit 11

Exercise 11.1

1 서울이에요. "(It) is Seoul."
2 토쿄예요. "(It) is Tokyo."
3 베이징이에요. "(It) is Beijing."
4 로마예요. "(It) is Rome."
5 카이로예요. "(It) is Cairo."
6 런던이에요. "(It) is London."
7 와싱턴이에요. "(It) is Washington."
8 뱅쿠버예요. "(It) is Vancouver."
9 상파울로예요. "(It) is Sao Paulo."
10 베를린이에요. "(It) is Berlin."

Exercise 11.2

1 바바라는 의사가 아니에요.
2 리처드는 대학생이 아니에요.
3 에릭은 디자이너가 아니에요.
4 씬디는 경찰이 아니에요.
5 이사벨은 기자가 아니에요.
6 데니엘은 외교관이 아니에요.
7 조지는 회계사가 아니에요.
8 사이몬은 과학자가 아니에요.
9 에비게일은 사업가가 아니에요.
10 다이에나는 간호사가 아니에요.

Exercise 11.3

1 존은 선생님이에요.
2 샌드라는 선생님이 아니에요.
3 피터는 의사예요.
4 메리는 의사가 아니에요.
5 리사는 엔지니어예요.
6 스티브는 엔지니어가 아니에요.
7 벤은 간호사예요.
8 린다는 간호사가 아니에요.
9 낸시는 대학생이에요.
10 찰스는 대학생이 아니에요.

Exercise 11.4

1 차이나타운이 샌프란시스코에 있어요.
2 바티칸이 이탈리아에 있어요.
3 상하이가 중국에 있어요.
4 그랜드캐년이 아리조나에 있어요.
5 디지니월드가 플로리다에 있어요.
6 피라미드가 이집트에 있어요.
7 아마존이 브라질에 있어요.
8 에베레스트산이 네팔에 있어요.
9 에펠타워가 파리에 있어요.
10 할리우드가 캘리포니아에 있어요.

Exercise 11.5

1 "As for Maria, (she) has a classical guitar."
2 "As for Annie, (she) has a keyboard."
3 "As for James, (he) has a bass guitar."

4 "As for Paul, (he) has a drum."
5 "As for Elisha, (she) has a violin."
6 "As for Eric, (he) has a saxophone."
7 "As for Robert, (he) has a clarinet."
8 "As for Kevin, (he) has a trumpet."
9 "As for Lisa, (she) has a piano."
10 "As for Joanne, (she) has a cello."

Exercise 11.6

1 제리는 돈이 있어요.
2 바바라는 열쇠가 있어요.
3 저스틴은 그림이 있어요.
4 가브리엘은 꽃이 있어요.
5 아담은 모자가 있어요.
6 리사는 빵이 있어요.
7 윌리엄은 고양이가 있어요.
8 해리는 우산이 있어요.
9 휴는 신문이 있어요.
10 다이엔은 자동차가 있어요.
11 조지는 자전거가 있어요.
12 나오미는 개가 있어요.

Exercise 11.7

1 위	2 뒤	3 밑	4 옆
5 앞	6 안	7 왼쪽	8 오른쪽

Unit 12

Exercise 12.1

1 빨래를 해요. "(I) do laundry."
2 외식을 해요. "(I) dine out."
3 설거지를 해요. "(I) wash dishes."
4 요리를 해요. "(I) cook."
5 세수를 해요. "(I) wash (my) faces."
6 이야기를 해요. "(I) talk."
7 산책을 해요. "(I) take a walk."
8 청소를 해요. "(I) clean."
9 전화를 해요. "(I) make phone calls."
10 숙제를 해요. "(I) do homework."

Exercise 12.2

1 매일 에어로빅을 해요.
2 매일 샤워를 해요.
3 매일 숙제를 해요.
4 매일 쇼핑을 해요.
5 매일 요가를 해요.
6 매일 전화를 해요.

Exercise 12.3

1 재즈를 좋아해요.
2 조깅을 좋아해요.
3 코미디를 좋아해요.
4 오렌지를 좋아해요.
5 파랑색을 좋아해요.
6 튤립을 좋아해요.
7 SUV를 좋아해요.

Exercise 12.4

1 "(I) memorize names."
2 "(I) win a game."
3 "(I) read a book."
4 "(I) keep a promise."
5 "(I) give water to the flower."
6 "(I) take a picture."
7 "(I) look for a key."
8 "(I) sell a bicycle."
9 "(I) smoke a cigarette."
10 "(I) wave hands."

Exercise 12.5

1 피터가 도서관에서 책을 읽어요.
2 존이 얼굴을 씻어요.
3 앤지가 스타벅스에서 커피를 마셔요.
4 매튜가 기숙사에서 텔레비전을 봐요.
5 윌리엄이 빵을 먹어요.
6 힐라리가 친구를 만나요.
7 조지가 꽃을 사요.
8 크리스가 한국어를 배워요.
9 캐서린이 이메일을 써요.
10 이사벨이 한국문화를 공부해요.

Exercise 12.6

1 으로	2 로	3 로	4 로	5 로	6 로	7 으로
8 로	9 로	10 으로	11 로	12 으로	13 로	14 으로

Exercise 12.7

1 "(I) open the door with a key."
2 "(I) go to New York by airplane."
3 "(I) will drink black coffee."
4 "(I) bought a white uniform."
5 "(I) go to Boston on Saturday."
6 "Please sit to the right side."
7 "Please change (this) with a blue ball-point pen."
8 "(I) bought a bigger car."
9 "As for noodles, (I) eat (them), using chopsticks."
10 "As for honeymoon, (we) will go to Las Vegas."

Unit 13

Exercise 13.1

1 Scott's car
2 Grace's ring
3 Ted's credit card
4 Linda's camera
5 Juliet's clothes
6 Edward's father
7 Robert's wallet
8 Jaclyn's money
9 Natalie's
10 Jane's

Exercise 13.2

1 토마스의 컴퓨터
2 애니의 열쇠
3 조앤의 펜
4 앤드류의 물
5 로미오의 사진
6 켄의 방
7 데이엘의 시계
8 사만다의 모자
9 캐렌의 사과
10 다이애나의 자전거

Exercise 13.3

1 책상이 교실에 있어요.
2 지갑이 차에 있어요.
3 카메라가 집에 있어요.
4 책이 학교에 있어요.
5 수잔이 서울에 있어요.
6 토마스가 런던에 있어요.
7 에펠타워가 파리에 있어요.
8 그랜드캐년이 아리조나에 있어요.
9 할리우드가 캘리포니아에 있어요.
10 피라미드가 이집트에 있어요.

Exercise 13.4

1 도서관에 가요
2 교실에 가요
3 공항에 가요
4 친구 집에 가요
5 교회에 가요
6 서점에 가요
7 병원에 가요
8 캔디 가게에 가요
9 약국에 가요
10 호텔에 가요

Exercise 13.5

1 <u>친구랑</u> 이야기해요.
2 <u>사무엘이랑</u> 운동 해요.
3 <u>제니퍼랑</u> 에어로빅 해요.
4 <u>데니엘이랑</u> 요리해요.
5 <u>이사벨이랑</u> 쇼핑 해요.
6 <u>제임스랑</u> 공부해요.
7 <u>캐서린이랑</u> 전화 해요.
8 <u>가족이랑</u> 외식 해요.
9 <u>피터랑</u> 청소해요.
10 <u>선생님이랑</u> 노래해요.

Exercise 13.6

1 커피하고 녹차가 있어요.
2 한국 사람하고 중국 사람이 있어요.
3 기타하고 드럼이 있어요.
4 악어하고 하마가 있어요.

5 개하고 고양이가 있어요.
6 사과하고 오렌지가 있어요.
7 빵하고 우유가 있어요.
8 컴퓨터하고 프린터가 있어요.
9 책상하고 의자가 있어요.
10 형하고 누나가 있어요.

Exercise 13.7

1 중국과 일본 "China and Japan"
2 봄과 가을 "Spring and Autumn"
3 소프라노와 알토 "soprano and alto"
4 사자와 하이에나 "lions and hyenas"
5 전쟁과 평화 "war and peace"
6 하늘과 땅 "sky and earth"
7 산과 바다 "mountain and sea"
8 남자와 여자 "man and woman"
9 불과 물 "fire and water"
10 물과 기름 "water and oil"

Unit 14

Exercise 14.1

1 에서	2 에	3 에서	4 에	5 에서
6 에서	7 에서	8 에서	9 에	10 에서

Exercise 14.2

1 에	2 한테서	3 께	4 에	5 한테서
6 한테	7 한테	8 에	9 에게	10 에게서

Exercise 14.3

1 마이클한테서 초대를 받았어요.
2 호텔에서 몇 시에 나갔어요?
3 그 이야기를 라디오에서 들었어요.
4 어제 앤드류한테 전화를 했어요.
5 지난 주에 김실장님께 멜을 보냈습니다.
6 쓰리기통에 쓰레기를 버리십시오.
7 앤드류한테서 책을 빌려요.
8 친구한테서 소식을 들어요.
9 집에 전화했어요.
10 한국 사람들한테 차를 팔아요.

Exercise 14.4

1 한국에서 편지가 왔어요.
2 학교 식당에서 친구를 만나요.
3 할아버지께 전화하세요.
4 선생님이 저한테 책을 주셨어요.
5 저스틴이 니콜한테 꽃을 주었어요.
6 저에게 (or 한테) 연락하세요.
7 학생들한테 (or 에게) 비디오를 보여 주세요.
8 부모님한테서 (or 에게서) 편지가 왔어요.

Exercise 14.5

1 은	2 에, 이	3 이, 의	4 의	5 에서	6 한테
7 한테서	8 에, 에	9 는, 에서	10 에	11 에서	12 에

Exercise 14.6

1 편지가 한국에서 도착했어요.
2 어머니한테 전화를 해요.
3 존한테서 책을 빌렸어요.
4 미국 학생들한테 한국어를 가르쳤어요.
5 친구한테 한국어로 말하세요?

Unit 15

Exercise 15.1

1 피아노도 쳐요. "(I) also play piano."
2 축구도 해요. "(I) also play soccer."
3 에어로빅도 해요. "(I) also do aerobics."
4 가난한 사람도 도와요. "(I) also help poor people."
5 노래도 불러요. "(I) also sing a song."
6 춤도 춰요. "(I) also dance."
7 손님도 많아요. "There are many customers as well."
8 음식도 맛있어요. "The food is delicious too."
9 방도 조용해요. "The room is also quiet."
10 바지도 비싸요. "The pants are also expensive."

Exercise 15.2

1 녹차만 마셔요. "(I) only drink green tea."
2 야채만 먹어요. "(I) only eat vegetables."
3 클래식 음악만 들어요. "(I) only listen to classical music."

4 코미디 영화만 봐요. "(I) only see comedy movies."
5 청바지만 입어요. "(I) only wear jeans."
6 주말만 쉬어요. "(I) rest only at the weekend."
7 방만 깨끗해요. "Only the room is clean."
8 한국 음식만 맛있어요. "Only Korean food is delicious."
9 화장실만 작아요. "Only the restroom is small."
10 싸게만 팔아요. "(They) sell (it) only at a cheap price."

Exercise 15.3

1 "As for Andrew, (he) likes only meat."
2 "As for Annie, (she) also has a Japanese car."
3 "As for James, (he) also bought a bass guitar."
4 "As for Paul, (he) also plays a drum."
5 "Only Elisha has the passport."
6 "Only Eric skis."
7 "Only Caroline uses a notebook."
8 "Only Richard went to school."
9 "Only Laurence is a student."
10 "Only Glen likes red wines."

Exercise 15.4

1 한국 사람만 있어요.
2 이 책도 수잔 거예요?
3 시계만 샀어요.
4 소설책도 좋아해요.
5 포장지도 예뻐요.
6 10 분만 더 기다리십시오.
7 가격도 싸요.
8 저 사람만 한국 사람이에요.
9 콜라만 주세요.
10 존은 아침에만 조깅을 해요.

Exercise 15.5

1 <u>커피도</u> 마셔요.
2 <u>매튜는</u> <u>베이스 기타만</u> 쳐요.
3 <u>도서관도</u> 집에서 가까워요.
4 <u>크리스틴만</u> 만날 거예요.
5 <u>신분증도</u> 지갑에서 꺼냈어요.
6 <u>타이어만</u> 새 것으로 갈았어요.
7 <u>휴지만</u> 쓰레기통에 버리세요.
8 <u>옷 색도</u> 예뻐요.

9 <u>가격도</u> 싸요.
10 <u>서비스도</u> 좋았어요.

Unit 16

Exercise 16.1

1 이나	2 이나	3 나	4 나	5 나
6 나	7 이나	8 이	9 나	10 나

Exercise 16.2

1 두 시간이나 운전했어요.
2 학교에 몇 사람이나 올까요?
3 집에서 스파게티나 만들래요.
4 캐나다나 영국으로 가고 싶어요.
5 한국음식은 무엇이나 잘 먹어요.

Exercise 16.3

1 남자나 여자 "a man or a woman"
2 뉴욕이나 런던 "New York or London"
3 영화나 드라마 "movie or drama"
4 할머니나 할아버지 "a grandmother or a grandfather"
5 딸이나 아들 "a daughter or a son"
6 비누나 샴푸 "soap or shampoo"
7 젓가락이나 숟가락 "chopsticks or spoons"
8 스파게티나 파스타 "spaghetti or pasta"
9 택시나 버스 "taxi or bus"
10 소파나 의자 "sofa or chair"

Exercise 16.4

1 가방이나 지갑
2 공항이나 기차역
3 꽃이나 카드
4 맥주나 와인
5 물이나 슈스
6 백화점이나 슈퍼마켓
7 빵이나 케이크
8 산이나 강
9 연필이나 펜
10 가족이나 친구

Exercise 16.5

1 "From the hospital to school."
2 "From evening till morning."
3 "From the airport to the hotel."
4 "From morning till night."
5 "From London to Paris."
6 "From the church to home."
7 "From the bank to the police station."
8 "From the post office to the coffee shop."
9 "From 10 a.m. till 2 p.m."
10 "From the pharmacy to the restaurant."

Exercise 16.6

1 커피까지 마셨어요. "(I) even drank coffee."
2 설거지까지 했어요. "(I) even did dishwashing."
3 에어로빅까지 했어요. "(I) even did aerobics."
4 보스톤까지 운전했어요. "(I) drive as far as (up to) Boston."
5 윌리엄까지 파티에 왔어요. "Even William came to the party."
6 타이어까지 바꿨어요. "(I) even changed tires."
7 전화까지 고장이에요. "Even the telephone is out of order."
8 신발까지 사고 싶어요. "(I) even want to buy shoes."
9 누나까지 만났어요. "(I) even met the older sister."
10 날씨까지 더웠어요. "Even the weather was hot."

Unit 17

Exercise 17.1

1 식탁에 수박이 있었어요. "There were watermelons on the dining table."
2 냉장고에 오렌지가 있었어요. "There were oranges in the refrigerator."
3 엔지가 약사였어요. "Angie was a pharmacist."
4 줄리가 헤어 디자이너였어요. "Julie was a hair designer."
5 오후 5 시에 도서관에서 나갔어요. "(I) went out from the library at 5 p.m."
6 아침 10 시에 버스를 탔어요. "(I) took the bus at 10 o'clock in the morning."
7 오후 9 시에 가게를 닫았어요. "(I) closed the store at 9 p.m."
8 일을 오후 6 시에 마쳤어요. "(I) finished the work at 6 p.m."
9 친구한테서 자전거를 빌렸어요. "(I) borrowed a bicycle from the friend."
10 화장실에서 손을 씻었어요. "(I) washed (my) hands at the restroom."

11 모자를 썼어요. "(I) am wearing a cap."
12 집에 왔어요. "(I) am home."
13 해가 떴어요. "The sun is up."
14 넥타이를 맸어요. "(I) am wearing a tie."

Exercise 17.2

1 유니폼을 입었었어요. "(I) used to wear a uniform."
2 서점에서 한국어 책을 팔았었어요. "(I) used to sell Korean books at the bookstore."
3 밤에 쓰레기를 버렸었어요. "(I) used to throw away garbage at night."
4 이 옷은 비쌌었어요. "As for this dress, (it) used to be expensive."
5 제니퍼의 집이 좋았었어요. "Jennifer's house was good (long before)."
6 한국 노래를 좋아했었어요. "(I) used to like Korean songs."
7 샘이 엔지니어였었어요. "Sam was an engineer (long before)."
8 이 집에서 요리를 했었어요. "(I) used to cook in this house."
9 야구를 했었어요. "(I) used to play baseball."
10 한국어를 배웠었어요. "(I) learned Korean (long before)."

Exercise 17.3

1 친구하고 포도주를 마셔요.
2 방이 더러워요.
3 날씨가 맑아요.
4 고마워요.
5 친구한테서 꽃을 받아요.
6 기차로 4 시간 걸려요.
7 인터넷으로 아버지한테 전화해요.
8 커피숍에서 만나요.
9 노래를 잘 해요.
10 안경을 써요.

Exercise 17.4

1 우리는 녹차를 마셨었어요.
2 클래식 음악을 들었어요.
3 양복을 입었어요.
4 방이 조용했어요.
5 호텔이 쌌었어요.
6 싸게 팔았었어요.
7 집에 왔어요.
8 커피가 맛있었어요.
9 야구를 좋아했었어요.
10 스칼릿이 영어 선생님이었었어요.

Unit 18

Exercise 18.1

1 김치를 안 사요. "(I) do not buy kimchi."
2 저녁을 안 먹어요. "(I) do not eat dinner."
3 물을 안 마셔요. "(I) do not drink water."
4 방을 청소 안 해요. "(I) do not clean the room."
5 구두를 안 신어요. "(I) do not wear shoes."
6 주말에 안 바빠요. "(I) am not busy on the weekend."
7 오늘은 안 추워요. "As for today, (it) is not cold."
8 방이 안 커요. "The room is not big."
9 음식이 안 짜요. "The food is not salty."
10 야채가 안 비싸요. "The vegetable is not expensive."

Exercise 18.2

1 내일 파티에 못 가요. "(I) cannot go to the party tomorrow."
2 도서관에서 책을 못 빌려요. "(I) cannot borrow the book from the library."
3 김치를 못 먹어요. "(I) cannot eat kimchi."
4 아버지한테 전화 못 해요. "(I) cannot make a phone call to father."
5 안경을 못 써요. "(I) cannot wear glasses."
6 넥타이를 못 매요. "(I) cannot wear a necktie."
7 비행기를 못 타요. "(I) cannot take an airplane."
8 운동을 못 해요. "(I) cannot do sports."
9 주말에 못 쉬어요. "(I) cannot rest on the weekend."
10 문을 못 열어요. "(I) cannot open the door."

Exercise 18.3

1 아니오, 배우지 않아요. "No, (I) do not learn (it)."
2 아니오, 어렵지 않아요. "No, (it) is not difficult."
3 아니오, 일하지 않아요. "No, (I) do not work."
4 아니오, 따뜻하지 않아요. "No, (it) is not warm."
5 아니오, 고프지 않아요. "No, (I) am not hungry."
6 아니오, 피곤하지 않아요. "No, (I) am not tired."
7 아니오, 좋아하지 않아요. "No, (I) do not like (it)."
8 아니오, 마시지 않았어요. "No, (I) did not drink (it)."
9 아니오, 만나지 않았어요. "No, (I) did not meet (him/her)."
10 아니오, 보지 않았어요. "No, (I) did not see (it)."

Exercise 18.4

1 쓰레기를 버리지 마십시오. "Don't throw away the garbage."
2 담배를 피우지 마십시오. "Don't smoke cigarettes."
3 술을 마시지 마십시오. "Don't drink liquor."
4 길을 건너지 마십시오. "Don't cross the road."
5 운전을 하지 마십시오. "Don't drive."
6 낮잠을 자지 마십시오. "Don't take a nap."
7 노래를 부르지 마십시오. "Don't sing a song."
8 얼굴을 씻지 마십시오. "Don't wash (your) face."
9 약을 먹지 마십시오. "Don't take the medicine."
10 크게 말하지 마십시오. "Don't speak aloud."

Exercise 18.5

1 늦게 일어나지 맙시다. "(Let us) not get up late."
2 내일 만나지 맙시다. "(Let us) not meet tomorrow."
3 커피를 마시지 맙시다. "(Let us) not drink coffee."
4 편지를 보내지 맙시다. "(Let us) not mail out the letter."
5 차를 팔지 맙시다. "(Let us) not sell the car."
6 옷을 사지 맙시다. "(Let us) not buy the dress."
7 동전을 넣지 맙시다. "(Let us) not insert the coin."
8 병원에 가지 맙시다. "(Let us) not go to the hospital."
9 요가를 하지 맙시다. "(Let us) not do yoga."
10 학교 식당 음식을 먹지 맙시다. "(Let us) not eat school cafeteria food."

Exercise 18.6

1 이름을 몰라요.
2 커피가 맛없어요.
3 책이 없어요.
4 아버지를 안 만났어요.
5 날씨가 안 추워요.
6 차를 팔지 맙시다.

Exercise 18.7

1 안 공부해요.
2 날씨가 못 추워요.
3 영화를 보지 않아요.
4 어제 수영 못 했어요.
5 방이 깨끗해요.
6 집에 갔어요.

Unit 19

Exercise 19.1

1 선생님한테 묻습니다. "(I) ask the teacher."
2 고기를 굽습니다. "(I) roast the meat."
3 책이 무겁습니다. "The book is heavy."
4 꽃병에 물을 붓습니다. "(I) pour water into a flower vase."
5 하늘이 파랗습니다. "The sky is blue."
6 강아지를 기릅니다. "(I) raise a puppy."
7 스파게티를 만듭니다. "(I) make spaghetti."
8 서울에서 삽니다. "(I) live in Seoul."
9 공이 물에 뜹니다. "The ball floats on the water."
10 배가 고픕니다. "(I) am hungry (lit. the stomach is empty)."

Exercise 19.2

1 친구하고 길을 걸어요. "(I) walk the road with friends."
2 어머니한테서 돈을 받아요. "(I) receive money from mother."
3 가방이 가벼워요. "The bag is light."
4 껌을 씹어요. "(I) chew a gum."
5 건물을 지어요. "(I) construct a building."
6 코트를 벗어요. "(I) take off a coat."
7 얼굴이 까매요. "The face is jet-black."
8 짐을 날라요. "(I) carry luggage."
9 커피를 팔아요. "(I) sell coffee."
10 수잔이 바빠요. "Susan is busy."

Exercise 19.3

1 듣다
2 밀다
3 차갑다
4 아름답다
5 긋다
6 하얗다
7 바르다
8 불다
9 예쁘다
10 아프다

Exercise 19.4

1 트렁크에 가방을 실어요.
2 머리가 어지러워요.
3 김치가 매워요.
4 방이 어두워요.
5 병이 나아요.
6 모자 색이 노래요.
7 노래를 불러요.
8 공항이 집에서 멉니다.
9 코트는 벽에 겁니다.
10 요즘 바빠요.

Unit 20

Exercise 20.1

1 일을 끝내고 싶어요. "(I) want to finish the work."
2 밖에 나가고 싶어요. "(I) want to go out to the outside."
3 영어를 가르치고 싶어요. "(I) want to teach English."
4 돈을 많이 벌고 싶어요. "(I) want to earn a lot of money."
5 병원에 가고 싶어요. "(I) want to go to the hospital."
6 'A'를 받고 싶어요. "(I) want to receive 'A'."
7 친구를 사귀고 싶어요. "(I) want to make friends."
8 집에서 쉬고 싶어요. "(I) want to rest at home."
9 운동을 하고 싶어요. "(I) want to exercise."
10 버스를 타고 싶어요. "(I) want to ride the bus."

Exercise 20.2

1 마리아가 대학교에 다니고 싶어해요. "Maria wants to attend the college."
2 스티븐이 의사가 되고 싶어해요. "Steven wants to become a medical doctor."
3 알렉스가 할머니를 만나고 싶어해요. "Alex wants to meet the grandmother."
4 리사가 오렌지 주스를 마시고 싶어해요. "Lisa wants to drink orange juice."
5 로라가 코트를 벗고 싶어해요. "Laura wants to take off (her) coat."
6 데이빗이 자동차를 사고 싶어해요. "David wants to buy a car."
7 니콜라스가 돈을 모으고 싶어해요. "Nicolas wants to save money."
8 레이첼이 친구를 돕고 싶어해요. "Rachel wants to help friends."
9 조셉이 친구 말을 믿고 싶어해요. "Joseph wants to believe the friend's word."
10 루이스가 한국어를 배우고 싶어해요. "Luis wants to learn Korean."

Exercise 20.3

1 손을 씻고 싶어요.
2 한국 노래를 듣고 싶어요.
3 서울에서 살고 싶어요.
4 A 를 받고 싶었어요.
5 한국어로 말하고 싶었어요.
6 택시를 타고 싶어해요.
7 책을 빌리고 싶어했어요.
8 쉬고 싶어해요.
9 스테이크를 주문하고 싶어했어요.
10 한국 노래를 부르고 싶어해요.

Exercise 20.4

1 매튜는 집에서 자고 있어요. "As for Matthew, (he) is sleeping at home."
2 우체국에서 편지를 부치고 있어요. "(I) am sending the letter at the post office."
3 친구의 자동차를 운전하고 있어요. "(I) am driving the friend's car."
4 부엌에서 음식을 만들고 있어요. "(I) am making food in the kitchen."
5 물을 끓이고 있어요. "(I) am boiling the water."
6 아버지를 기다리고 있어요. "(I) am waiting for father."
7 사람들의 의견을 모으고 있어요. "(I) am gathering people's opinions."
8 밖에서 놀고 있어요. "(I) am playing outside."
9 얼굴을 씻고 있어요. "(I) am washing (my) face."
10 바지를 입고 있어요. "(I) am wearing pants."

Exercise 20.5

1 에리카가 존을 도서관에서 만나고 있어요.
2 브라이언이 교수님한테 전화를 하고 있어요.
3 메건이 백화점에서 옷을 고르고 있어요.
4 아론이 킴벌리하고 영화를 보고 있어요.
5 데니엘 집에서 피자를 먹고 있어요.
6 형하고 커피를 마시고 있었어요.
7 우리 팀이 이기고 있어요.
8 가라오케에서 노래를 부르고 있었어요.
9 할아버지가 조깅을 하고 계세요.
10 아버지가 회사에서 일하고 계세요.

Unit 21

Exercise 21.1

1 저는 야구를 할 거예요.
2 저는 피아노를 칠 거예요.
3 우리는 태권도를 배울 거예요.
4 줄리는 에어로빅을 할 거예요.
5 리사는 일을 끝낼 거예요.
6 킴벌리는 학교 운동장에서 뛸 거예요.
7 사라는 집에 있을 거예요.
8 데이빗은 친구를 기다릴 거예요.
9 로렌은 물을 끓일 거예요.
10 폴은 돈을 모을 거예요.

Exercise 21.2

1 공항에서 택시를 탈 거예요. "(I) will (probably) ride the taxi at the airport."
2 한국어를 가르칠 거예요. "(I) will (probably) teach Korean."
3 다음 주에 일을 그만둘 거예요. "(I) will (probably) quit (my) job next week."
4 친구들이랑 집에서 놀 거예요. "(I) will (probably) play at home with friends."
5 형의 말을 믿을 거예요. "(I) will (probably) believe the older brother's words."
6 친구의 생일 파티에 갈 거예요. "(I) will (probably) go to the friend's birthday party."
7 내일 날씨는 추울 거예요. "As for tomorrow's weather, (it) will (probably) be cold."
8 아침에 조깅 할 거예요. "(I) will (probably) jog in the morning."
9 제이슨은 바쁠 거예요. "As for Jason, (he) will (probably) be busy."
10 화장품을 살 거예요. "(I) will (probably) buy the cosmetics."

Exercise 21.3

1 살다	2 듣다	3 맵다	4 돕다	5 낫다
6 파랗다	7 부르다	8 알다	9 벌다	10 고프다

Exercise 21.4

1 일레인이 가수일 거예요. "Elaine is probably a singer."
2 찰스가 엔지니어일 거예요. "Charles is probably an engineer."
3 리디아가 의사일 거예요. "Lydia is probably a medical doctor."

4 제이슨이 기자일 거예요. "Jason is probably a journalist."
5 엔지가 약사일 거예요. "Angie is probably a pharmacist."
6 브라이언이 회사원일 거예요. "Brian is probably an office worker."
7 줄리가 간호사일 거예요. "Julie is probably a nurse."
8 사이몬이 목수일 거예요. "Simon is probably a carpenter."
9 이사벨이 앵커우먼일 거예요. "Isabel is probably an anchor woman."
10 톰이 배우일 거예요. "Tom is probably an actor."

Exercise 21.5

1 "Shall I buy the bread?"
2 "Shall I sleep in this room?"
3 "Shall I cook?"
4 "Shall we take a taxi?"
5 "Shall we help that friend?"
6 "Do (you) think that the weather will be cloudy?"
7 "Do (you) think that the food will be delicious?"
8 "Do (you) think that the dress will be expensive?"
9 "Do (you) think that Eric will learn Taekwondo?"
10 "Do (you) think that Jessica will come to New York?"

Exercise 21.6

1 선생님이 재즈를 들을까요? "Do (you) think that the teacher will listen to jazz?"
2 애니가 일본 차를 좋아할까요? "Do (you) think that Annie will like Japanese cars?"
3 제임스가 축구를 할까요? "Do (you) think that James will play soccer?"
4 앨리스가 전화할까요? "Do (you) think that Alice will make a phone call?"
5 로렌스가 기차를 탈까요? "Do (you) think that Laurence will ride a train?"
6 글렌이 와인을 마실까요? "Do (you) think that Glen will drink wine?"
7 집이 조용할까요? "Do (you) think that the house will be quiet?"
8 백화점이 붐빌까요? "Do (you) think that the department store will be crowded?"
9 날씨가 더울까요? "Do (you) think that the weather will be hot?"
10 거리가 깨끗할까요? "Do (you) think that the street will be clean?"

Unit 22

Exercise 22.1

　1 T　　　2 F　　　3 F　　　4 T　　　5　T

Exercise 22.2

　1 새　　2 헌　　3 딴　　4 맨　　5 옛
　6 새　　7 헌　　8 딴　　9 맨　　10 순

Exercise 22.3

　1 저 집　　　　2 이 시간　　　3 저 커피숍　　4 이 색
　5 그 교수님　　6 이 것　　　　7 그 것
　8 여기/이 곳　9 거기/그 곳　10 저기/저 곳

Exercise 22.4

　1 무슨　　2 어느　　3 무슨　　4 무슨
　5 무슨　　6 어느　　7 어느　　8 무슨

Unit 23

Exercise 23.1

　1 천천히　　2 매우　　3 가장　　4 너무　　　5 열심히
　6 함께　　　7 많이　　8 혼자서　9 잘　　　10 가까이

Exercise 23.2

　1 막　　　　2 보통　　　3 벌써　　4 이미
　5 드디어　　6 밤낮　　　7 이따　　8 당분간
　9 갑자기　10 요즈음　11 아직　12 아까

Exercise 23.3

　1 그래서　　2 그렇지만　3 그런데　4 그럼　　5 그래서
　6 그렇지만　7 그리고　　8 그래서　9 그러나　10 그러니까

Exercise 23.4

　1 외롭게 "lonesomely"
　2 위험하게 "dangerously"

3 우습게 "laughably"
4 쉽게 "easily"
5 시원하게 "refreshingly"
6 씩씩하게 "manly"
7 부드럽게 "softly"
8 느리게 "slowly"
9 궁금하게 "curiously"
10 맵게 "spicily"

Unit 24

Exercise 24.1

1 한국 영화를 볼래요. "(I) will (intend to) see a Korean movie."
2 일본 차를 살래요. "(I) will (intend to) buy a Japanese car."
3 미국에서 살래요. "(I) will (intend to) live in America."
4 누나의 이야기를 믿을래요. "(I) will (intend to) believe the older sister's story."
5 친구를 도울래요. "(I) will (intend to) help the friend."
6 손을 씻을래요. "(I) will (intend to) wash (my) hands."
7 친구를 기다릴래요. "(I) will (intend to) wait for the friend."
8 꽃병에 물을 줄래요. "(I) will (intend to) give water to the vase."
9 방학을 즐길래요. "(I) will (intend to) enjoy the vacation."
10 한국인 친구를 사귈래요. "(I) will (intend to) make Korean friends."

Exercise 24.2

1 집에 갈래요.
2 보스톤에서 살래요.
3 밤 11 시에 잘래요.
4 도서관에서 공부할래요.
5 부엌에서 만들래요.
6 파스타(를) 먹을래요.
7 한국 영화(를) 볼래요.
8 한국어(를) 배울래요.
9 아침 6 시에 일어날래요.
10 아버지를 만날래요.

Exercise 24.3

1 제가 차를 팔게요. "I will (promise to) sell the car."
2 제가 창문을 열게요. "I will (promise to) open the window."
3 제가 노래를 부를게요. "I will (promise to) sing a song."

4 제가 샐러드를 시킬게요. "I will (promise to) order the salad."
5 제가 도울게요. "I will (promise to) help."
6 제가 돈을 낼게요. "I will (promise to) pay the money."
7 제가 학교에 전화할게요. "I will (promise to) make a phone call to school."
8 제가 색을 고를게요. "I will (promise to) choose the color."
9 제가 편지를 부칠게요. "I will (promise to) mail out the letter."
10 제가 가게 문을 닫을게요. "I will (promise to) close the store door."

Exercise 24.4

1 "(I) will (probably) wear a suit."
2 "(I) will (promise to) contact the friend."
3 "I will (intend to) make hamburgers."
4 "(I) will (probably) sleep over the friend's house."
5 "(I) will (promise to) make a phone call this weekend."
6 "(I) will (intend to) quit the work."
7 "(I) will (promise to) get up early tomorrow."
8 "(I) will (intend to) sit in the front seat."
9 "(I) will (probably) talk to the teacher."
10 "(I) will (intend to) learn Taekwondo."

Unit 25

Exercise 25.1

1 제가 일을 금요일까지 마치겠습니다. "(I) will finish the work by Friday."
2 제가 매일 운동하겠습니다. "I will exercise everyday."
3 내일은 제가 지하철을 타겠습니다. "As for tomorrow, (I) will take a subway."
4 제가 저녁을 준비하겠습니다. "I will prepare the dinner."
5 제가 친구를 기다리겠습니다. "I will wait for the friend."
6 시험이 쉽겠습니다. "(I guess that) the test will be easy."
7 내일 날씨가 춥겠습니다. "(I guess that) tomorrow's weather will be cold."
8 드라마가 재미있겠습니다. "(I guess that) the drama will be interesting."
9 집 값이 비싸겠습니다. "(I guess that) the housing price will be expensive."
10 품질이 좋겠습니다. "(I guess that) the quality will be good."

Exercise 25.2

1 "Will (you) quit smoking?"
2 "Will (you) study hard?"
3 "(Do you think that) the house will be quiet?"
4 "(Do you think that) the food will be delicious?"
5 "(Do you think that) the road will be narrow?"
6 "As for tomorrow's weather, (do you think that) it will be hot?"
7 "(Do you think that) the room will be clean?"
8 "(Do you think that) Thomas took the bus?"
9 "(Do you think that) Isabel made a phone call?"
10 "(Do you think that) Jessica waited for (her) friend?"

Exercise 25.3

1 매일 에어로빅을 하겠습니다.
2 꼭 약속을 지키겠습니다.
3 꼭 열쇠를 찾겠습니다.
4 꼭 담배를 끊겠습니다.
5 꼭 집을 팔겠습니다.
6 내일은 흐리겠습니다.
7 내일은 비가 내리겠습니다.
8 내일은 바람이 많이 불겠습니다.
9 내일은 교통이 막히겠습니다.
10 내일은 길이 미끄럽겠습니다.

Exercise 25.4

1 길을 건너십니다. "(He) crosses the street."
2 골프를 치십니다. "(He) plays golf."
3 한국어를 가르치십니다. "(He) teaches Korean."
4 문을 두드리십니다. "(He) knocks on the door."
5 한국 영화를 보십니다. "(He) sees a Korean movie."
6 그 친구를 믿으십니다. "(He) believes that friend."
7 고등학교 선생님이십니다. "(He) is a high-school teacher."
8 점심을 잡수십니다. "(He) eats lunch."
9 거실에서 주무십니다. "(He) sleeps in the living room."
10 학교에 계십니다. "(He) is in school."

Index

Page numbers in **bold** refer to those sections in the book where the relevant grammar point is discussed in detail.

Colloquial Korean

Kim In-Seok

Colloquial Korean is easy to use and completely up-to-date!

Specially written by an experience teacher for self-study or class use, the course offers you a step-by-step approach to written and spoken Korean. No prior knowledge of the language is required.

What makes *Colloquial Korean* your best choice in personal language learning?

Interactive – lots of exercises for regular practice

Clear – Concise grammar notes

Practical – useful vocabulary and pronunciation guide

Complete – including answer key and reference section

By the end of this rewarding course you will be able to communicate confidently and effectively in Korean in a broad range of everyday situations.

Two 60-minute CDs are available to complement the book. Recorded by native speakers, this material will help develop your listening and pronunciation skills.

Pbk: 978-0-415-10804-1
CDs: 978-0-415-28691-6
Book and CDs course: 978-0-415-42700-5
Mp3: 978-0-415-47079-7